DOMESDAY BOOK

Surrey

History from the Sources

DOMESDAY BOOK

A Survey of the Counties of England

LIBER DE WINTONIA

Compiled by direction of

KING WILLIAM I

Winchester
1086

DOMESDAY BOOK

text and translation edited by

JOHN MORRIS

3

Surrey

edited from a draft translation prepared by

Sara Wood

PHILLIMORE
Chichester
1975

1975

Published by

PHILLIMORE & CO. LTD.,
London and Chichester

Head Office: Shopwyke Hall,
Chichester, Sussex, England

© John Morris, 1975

ISBN   0   85033   132   3
*Printed in Great Britain by
Titus Wilson & Son Ltd.
Kendal*

SURREY

History from the Sources
General Editor: John Morris

The series aims to publish history
written directly from the sources
for all interested readers, specialists
and others. The first priority is to
publish important texts which should
be widely available, but are not.

DOMESDAY BOOK

The contents, with the folio on which each county begins, are:

Domesday Book is termed *Liber de Wintonia* (The Book of Winchester) in column 332c

INTRODUCTION

The Domesday Survey

In 1066 Duke William of Normandy conquered England. He was crowned King, and most of the lands of the English nobility were soon granted to his followers. Domesday Book was compiled 20 years later. The Saxon Chronicle records that in 1085

> at Gloucester at midwinter ... the King had deep speech with his counsellors ... and sent men all over England to each shire ... to find out ... what or how much each landholder held ... in land and livestock, and what it was worth ... The returns were brought to him.[1]

William was thorough. One of his Counsellors reports that he also sent a second set of Commissioners 'to shires they did not know, where they were themselves unknown, to check their predecessors' survey, and report culprits to the King.[2]

The information was collected at Winchester, corrected, abridged, chiefly by omission of livestock and the 1066 population, and fair-copied by one writer into a single volume. Norfolk, Suffolk and Essex were copied, by several writers, into a second volume, unabridged, which states that 'the Survey was made in 1086'. The surveys of Durham and Northumberland, and of several towns, including London, were not transcribed, and most of Cumberland and Westmorland, not yet in England, was not surveyed. The whole undertaking was completed at speed, in less than 12 months, though the fair-copying of the main volume may have taken a little longer. Both volumes are now preserved at the Public Record Office. Some versions of regional returns also survive. One of them, from Ely Abbey,[3] copies out the Commissioners' brief. They were to ask

> The name of the place; Who held it, before 1066, and now? How many *hides*?[4]
> How many ploughs, both those in lordship and the men's?
> How many villagers, cottagers and slaves, how many free men and Freemen?[5]
> How much woodland, meadow and pasture? How many mills and fishponds?
> How much has been added or taken away? What the total value was and is?
> How much each free man or Freeman had or has? All threefold, before 1066, when King William gave it, and now; and if more can be had than at present?

The Ely volume also describes the procedure. The Commissioners took evidence on oath 'from the Sheriff; from all the barons and their Frenchmen; and from the whole Hundred, the priests, the reeves and six villagers from each village'. It also names four Frenchmen and four Englishmen from each Hundred, who were sworn to verify the detail.

The King wanted to know what he had, and who held it. The Commissioners therefore listed lands in dispute, for Domesday Book was not only a tax-assessment. To the King's grandson, Bishop Henry of Winchester, its purpose was that every 'man should know his right and not

[1] Before he left England for the last time, late in 1086.
[2] Robert Losinga, Bishop of Hereford 1079-1095 (see *E.H.R.* 22, 1907, 74).
[3] *Inquisitio Eliensis*, folio 1a.
[4] A land unit.
[5] *Quot liberi homines? Quot sochemani?*

usurp another's'; and because it was the final authoritative register of rightful possession 'the natives called it Domesday Book, by analogy from the Day of Judgement'; that was why it was carefully arranged by Counties, and by landholders within Counties, 'numbered consecutively ... for easy reference'.[6]

Domesday Book describes Old English society under new management, in minute statistical detail. Foreign lords had taken over, but little else had yet changed. The chief landholders and those who held from them are named, and the rest of the population was counted. Most of them lived in villages, whose houses might be clustered together, or dispersed among their fields. Villages were grouped in administrative districts called Hundreds, which formed regions within Shires, or Counties, which survive today with minor boundary changes; the recent deformation of some ancient county identities is here disregarded, as are various short-lived modern changes. The local assemblies, though overshadowed by lords great and small, gave men a voice, which the Commissioners heeded. Very many holdings were described by the Norman term *manerium* (manor), greatly varied in size and structure from tiny farmsteads to vast holdings; and many lords exercised their own jurisdiction and other rights, termed *soca*, whose meaning still eludes exact definition.

The survey was unmatched in Europe for many centuries, the product of a sophisticated and experienced English administration, fully exploited by the Conqueror's commanding energy. But its unique assemblage of facts and figures has been hard to study, because the text has not been easily available, and abounds in technicalities. Investigation has therefore been chiefly confined to specialists; a wide range of questions cannot be tackled adequately without a cheap text and uniform translation available to a wider range of students, including local historians.

Previous Editions

The text of the two volumes has been printed once, in 1783 by Abraham Farley, in an edition of 1,250 copies, at Government cost, originally estimated at £18,000 exclusive of salaries. Its preparation took 16 years. It was set in a specially designed type, destroyed by fire in 1808, here reproduced from the original edition. In 1816 the Records Commissioners added two more volumes, edited by Sir Henry Ellis, of introduction, indices, and associated text; and in 1861-1863 the Ordnance Survey issued zincograph facsimiles of the whole. Separate texts of many counties have appeared since 1673 and separate translations in the Victoria County Histories and elsewhere.

This Edition

Farley's text is used, because of its excellence, and because any worthy alternative would prove astronomically expensive. His text has been checked against the facsimile, and discrepancies observed have been

[6] *Dialogue de Scaccario*, 1, 16.

verified against the manuscript, by the kindness of Miss Daphne Gifford of the Public Record Office. Farley's few errors are indicated in the notes.

The editor is responsible for the translation and lay-out. It aims at what the compiler would have written if his language had been modern English; though no translation can be exact, for even a simple word like 'free' nowadays means freedom from different restrictions. Bishop Henry emphasized that his grandfather preferred 'ordinary words'; the nearest ordinary modern English is therefore chosen whenever possible. Words that are now obsolete, or have changed their meaning, are avoided, but measurements have to be transliterated, since their extent is often unknown or arguable, and varied regionally. The terse inventory form of the original has been retained, as have the ambiguities of the Latin.

Modern English commands two main devices unknown to 11th-century Latin: standardised punctuation and paragraphs. Latin *ibi* (there are) is usually rendered by a full stop, Latin *et* (and) by a comma or semi-colon. The entries normally answer the Commissioners' questions, arranged in five main groups, (i) the place and its holder, its hides, ploughs and lordship; (ii) people; (iii) resources; (iv) value; and (v) additional notes. These groups are usually given as separate paragraphs.

King William numbered chapters 'for easy reference', and sections within chapters are commonly marked, usually by initial capitals, often edged in red. They are here numbered, for ease of reference only. Maps, indices and an explanation of technical terms are also given. Later, it is hoped to publish full analytical tables, an explanatory volume, and associated texts.

The editor is deeply indebted to the advice of many scholars, too numerous to name, and especially to the Public Record Office, and to the publisher's patience. The draft translations are the work of a team; they have been co-ordinated and corrected by the editor, and each has been checked by several people. It is therefore hoped that mistakes may be fewer than in versions published by single fallible individuals. But it would be Utopian to hope that the translation is altogether free from error; the editor would therefore like to be informed of mistakes observed.

Huntingdonshire, Middlesex and Surrey have been the experimental counties at all stages of this edition. They may therefore contain more ineptitudes and mistakes than other counties.

The texts have been set by Sheila Brookshire, Jill Doig, Yvonne Grant, Auriol Hyde Parker, Isobel Thompson and Elizabeth Thorney-croft. The map is the work of Jim Hardy.

Conventions

*   refers to a note.
[ ]   enclose words omitted in the MS.
( )   enclose editorial explanations.

S V D R I E.

HIC ANNOTANT TENENTES TRAS IN SVDRIE.

.I. Rex WILLELMVS.

.II. Archieps Cantuar.

.III. Eps Wintoniensis.

.IIII Eps Osbernus

.V. Eps Baiocensis

.VI. Abb de Westmonast.

.VII. Abb de Wintonia

.VIII. Abb de Certesy.

.IX. Abb S Wandregesili.

.X. Abb de Cruce S Leutfredi.

.XI. Abb de Labatailge.

.XII. Abbatissa de Berchinges.

.XIII. Canonici S. Pauli Lundon.

.XII. Æccla de Lantheige.

.XV. Comes Eustachius.

.XVI. Comitissa Bononiensis.

.XVII. Comes Moritoniensis.

.XVI. Comes Rogerius.

.XIX. Ricard de Tonebrige.

.XX. Wills de Braiose.

.XXI. Wills filius Ansculfi.

.XXII. Walterius filius Other.

.XXIII. Walterius de Douuai.

.XXII. Gislebt fili Richerii.

.XXV Goisfrid de Manneuile.

.XXVI. Goisfrid Orlateile.

.XXVII. Eduuard Sarisberie.

.XXVIII Robtus malet.

.XXIX. Milo crispin.

.XXX. Haimo uicecomes.

.XXXI. Hunfrid camerarius.

.XXXII. Radulf de felgeres.

.XXXIII. Rainald fili Erchebaldi.

.XXXII. Albertus clericus.

.XXXV. Odard balistarius.

.XXXVI. Osuuold Teodricus.

7 alii seruientes regis.

SURREY

LIST OF LANDHOLDERS IN SURREY

1 King William
2 The Archbishop of Canterbury
3 The Bishop of Winchester
4 Bishop Osbern
5 The Bishop of Bayeux
6 The Abbot* of Westminster
7 The Abbot of Winchester
8 The Abbot of Chertsey
9 The Abbot of St. Wandrille
10 The Abbot of [Holy] Cross, St. Leufroy
11 The Abbot of Battle
12 The Abbess of Barking
13 The Canons of St. Pauls London
14 Lambeth Church
15 Count Eustace
16 The Countess of Boulogne
17 The Count of Mortain
18 Earl Roger
19 Richard of Tonbridge
20 William of Braose
21 William son of Ansculf
22 Walter son of Othere
23 Walter of Douai
24 Gilbert son of Richere
25 Geoffrey de Mandeville
26 Geoffrey Orlateile
27 Edward of Salisbury
28 Robert Malet
29 Miles Crispin
30 Hamo the Sheriff
31 Humphrey the Chamberlain
32 Ralph of Feugeres
33 Reginald son of Erchenbald*
34 Albert the Clerk
35 Odard the Gunner
36 Oswald, Theodoric and others of the King's Servants

IN GILDEFORD HABET REX WILLELMVS . LXXV.

hagas . in quibʒ manent . CLXXV . homines.

T.R.E. reddeƀ . XVIII . liƀ 7 III . denar̃ . Modo ap̃pciat̃ . xxx.

liƀ . 7 tam̃ redd . XXXII . liƀ.

De fup̃dictis hagis hт̃ Rannulf⁹ cleric⁹ . III . hagas ubi maneɴ

VI . hões . 7 inde hт̃ ifd Rann̄ facā 7 focā . nifi cōmune geldū

in uilla uenerit unde null⁹ euadat . Si hõ ej⁹ in uilla delinqt

7 diuadiat⁹ euadat⁓ nil inde hт̃ p̃pofit⁹ regis . Si ů calūniat⁹ ibi

fuerit 7 diuadiat⁓ тc̃ hт̃ rex emendā . Sic tenuit eas Stigand᷄

᷄Rannulf᷄ teñ . I . hagā . quā hucufqʒ tenuit de ep̃o baiocfi.

Hões ů teftificant᷄ q̓a n̄ adjacet alicui manerio . fed qui teneƀ eā

T.R.E. conceffit eā Toui p̃pofito uillæ . p̃ em̃datione uni⁹ fuæ forisfacturæ.

᷄Altera dom⁹ . ē q̓ teñ p̃pofit⁹ epi baioc̃ de Cͦ Bronlei . De hoc dn̄t

hões de comitatu . qd n̄ hт̃ | aliā rectitudinē . nifi qd quandā ui

duā cuj⁹ erat dom⁹ accep̃ p̃pofit⁹ uillæ . 7 ido mifit ep̃s domū illā

in fuo Cͦ . 7 huc ufqʒ p̃didit rex c̃fuetudiñes . ep̃s auт̃ habet.

᷄Dn̄t etiā hões q̓ jurauer̃ de alia domo quæ jacet in Brun

lei . p̃pt᷄ hoc tantū qd p̃pofit de ipfa uilla fuit amicus hõis

illius qui hanc domū habebat . 7 eo mortuo c̃uertit eā ad Cͦ

᷄Walerann⁹ q̓qʒ defaifiuit qnendā hominē   ᷄de Bronlei.

de una domo unde rex . E . habeƀ c̃fuetudinē . Modo teñ

eā Otƀtus cū c̃fuetud fic dicit p regē . W.

Roƀt⁹ de Wateuile teñ . I . domū . quæ reddeƀ om̃em

c̃fuetud . T.R.E. modo nichil reddit.

1   LAND OF THE KING

In WOKING Hundred

1a In GUILDFORD King William has 75 sites, whereon dwell 175 men.
Before 1066 they paid £18 0s 3d; now they are assessed
at £30; however, they pay £32.

1b Ranulf Clerk has 3 of the above sites, where 6 men dwell.
Ranulf also has full jurisdiction therein, save when the common
tax comes upon the town, from which no man escapes.
If one of his men is apprehended for a crime in the town and
escapes, the King's reeve has nothing therefrom; but if he
should be charged and apprehended there, then the King has
the fine. Thus Archbishop Stigand held these (sites).

1c Ranulf the Sheriff holds one site which he held hitherto from
the Bishop of Bayeux. But the men (of the County) testify
that it is not included in any manor, but that before 1066 its
holder granted it to Tovi, the town reeve, in payment of one
of his fines.

1d There is another house which the reeve of the Bishop of
Bayeux holds from the manor of Bramley. Of this, the men of
the County state that he has no other right there, but that the
reeve of the village* took (in marriage) a widow, whose house
it was, and that therefore the Bishop put the house into his manor;
hitherto the King has lost its customary dues, but the Bishop
has them.

1e Of another house which lies in (the lands of) Bramley, the sworn
men (of the County) state that it is only because the reeve
of that village* was a friend of the man who had the house,
and on his death he transferred it to the manor of Bramley.

1f Waleran also dispossessed a man of a house from which King Edward
had customary dues. Now Odbert holds it, with customary dues,
through King William, as he says.

1g Robert of Watteville holds 1 house which paid all customary
dues before 1066; now it pays nothing.

Rex .W. ten in dnĩo *WOCHINGES* . De firma regis .E.
fuit . Tc̃ ſe defđ ᵽ. xv . hiđ 7 dim̃ . Nunq̃ geldaueꝛ . Tra . ē
vi . car̃ . In dnĩo . ē una . 7 xxxiii . uiłłi 7 ix . borđ cũ . xx . car̃ .
Ibi æccła . Osƀn tenet . 7 ibi . i . molin̄ de . xi . ſoł . 7 iiii . den̄ . Ibi
xxxii . ac̃ ᵱti . Silua꞉ de . cxxxiii .porc̃ .
De hac tra ten̄ Walt fili Otherii . iii . virg̃ . Hanc q̃dā foreſtar̃
tenuit . T . R . E . 7 tc̃ fuit poſita ext Maneꝛ . ᵱ rege . E . Ibi m̃ nichil . ē .

T . R . E . 7 poſt . ualuit . xv . liƀ ad numeꝛ . Modo . xv . liƀ ad penſũ .
7 uicecomiti . xxv . ſoł .

Rex ten̄ in dnĩo *STOCHÆ* . De firma regis . E . fuit . Tc̃ ſe defđ
ᵽ . xvii . hiđ . Nichil geldaueꝛ . Tra . ē . xvi . car̃ . In dnĩo ſunt
ii . car̃ . 7 xxiiii . uiłłi 7 x . borđ cũ . xx . car̃ . Ibi æccła . q̃ Wiłłs
ten̄ de rege cũ dimiđ hida in elemoſina . Ibi . v . ſerui . 7 ii . mo
lini de . xxv . ſoł . 7 xvi . ac̃ ᵱti . Silua꞉ xl . porc̃ . 7 ipſa . ē
in parco regis .

T . R . E . 7 poſt꞉ ualƀ . xii . liƀ . Modo꞉ xv . liƀ . Tam̃ qui ten̄
redđ . xv . liƀ ad penſũ . Vicecom̃ h̃t . xxv . ſoliđ .

In Brixistan hvnd.

Rex ten̄ *BERMVNDESYE* . Herald tenuit . Tc̃ ſe defđ
ᵽ . xiii . hiđ . m̃ ᵽ . xii . hiđ . Tra . ē . viii . car̃ . In dnĩo . ē una .
car̃ . 7 xxv . uiłłi 7 xxxiii . borđ cũ . iiii . car̃ .
Ibi ꝑoua 7 pulchra æccła . 7 xx . ac̃ ᵱti . Silua꞉ v . porc̃
de paſnag . In Lundonia . xiii . burḡſes de . xliiii . den̄ .
T . R . E . 7 m̃꞉ ual . xv . liƀ . 7 uiceco̅m̃ h̃t . xx . ſoł .
ꝟComes morit ten̄ . i . hidā quæ T . R . E . 7 poſt fuit in hoc m̃ .

2 King William holds WOKING in lordship. It was in King Edward's
revenue. Then it answered for 15½ hides; they never paid tax.
Land for 6 ploughs. In lordship 1;*
   33 villagers and 9 smallholders with 20 ploughs.
    A church;* Osbern holds it.
   1 mill at 11s 4d; meadow, 32 acres; woodland at 133 pigs.*
    Walter son of Othere holds 3 virgates of this land.
    A forester held it before 1066; it was then placed outside
    the manor, through King Edward. There is nothing there now.
Value before 1066 and later £15 at face value; now £15
by weight, and 25s to the Sheriff.

  The King holds*
3 STOKE (-by-Guildford), in lordship. It was in King Edward's
revenue. Then it answered for 17 hides; they paid nothing
in tax. Land for 16 ploughs. In lordship 2 ploughs;
   24 villagers and 10 smallholders with 20 ploughs.
    A church, which William holds from the King in alms
    with ½ hide. 5 slaves.
   2 mills at 25s; meadow, 16 acres; woodland, 40 pigs;*
    it is in the King's park.
Value before 1066 and later £12; now £15; however, its
holder pays £15 by weight. The Sheriff has 25s.

  In BRIXTON Hundred
4 BERMONDSEY. Earl Harold held it. Then it answered*
for 13 hides, now for 12 hides. Land for 8 ploughs.
In lordship 1 plough;
   25 villagers and 33 smallholders with 4 ploughs.
    A new and beautiful church*.
  Meadow, 20 acres; woodland, 5 pigs from pasturage.
    In London, 13 burgessess at 44d.
Value before 1066 and now £15; the Sheriff has 20s.
   The Count of Mortain holds 1 hide* which was in this manor
before 1066 and later.

Rex ten̄ *MERETONE*. Herald tenuit . T̄c se defd̄ 7 m̄ com
p̄ . xx . hid̄ . Tra . ē . xxi . car̄ . In dn̄io sunt . ii . car̄ . 7 lvi .
uilli 7 xiii . b̄ord cū . xviii . car̄ . Ibi æccła . 7 ii . molini
de . lx . soł . 7 x . ac̄ p̄ti . Silua: q̄t xx . porc̄ .
T.R.E. ualb̄ . xxv . lib̄ . 7 post: xvi . lib̄ . Modo: xxxv . lib̄ .
tam̄ qui ten̄ redd̄ . xliii . lib̄ . In Sudwerca . xvi . ma
suræ de . xviii . soł 7 ii . denar̄ . huic m̄ ptin̄ .
⌐Quidā Orcus ten̄ . ii . hid̄ quæ sēp̄ jacuer̄ in isto m̄ .
7 sunt in alio hund̄ . Ipse tenuit T.R.E. T̄c se defd̄ p̄ . ii .
hid̄ . m̄ p̄ nichilo . Ibi . i . car̄ in dn̄io . 7 ii . ac̄ p̄ti . Vał sēp̄ . xx . soł .
Eps Lisoiensis ten̄ in chent . ii . solins qui huic m̄
adjacuer̄ . T.R.E. 7 regis . W. sīc testant̄ hōes de hund̄ .
Ipse reclamat aduocat epm̄ baioc̄sem . 7 p̄posit suus
inde noluit placitare.

IN WALETON HVND.

Rex ten̄ in dn̄io *WALETONE* . T.R.E. 7 m̄ se defd̄
p̄ . xi . hid̄ . Tra . ē . xi . car̄ . In dn̄io . ē una car̄ . 7 xv .
uilli 7 xiiii . bord cū . x . car̄ . Ibi . iii . serui . 7 ii . molini
de . xxx . solid̄ . 7 viii . ac̄ p̄ti . Silua quæ . ē in Chent:
⌐Ricard de Tonebrige ten̄ de hoc m̄ unā uirgatā
cū silua . unde abstulit rusticū qui ibi manebat . N̄c
reddit uicecomiti . x . soł . p̄ annū .
Totū m̄ T.R.E. ualb̄ . xv . lib̄ . Modo: x . lib̄ .

IN CHERCHEFELLE HVND.

Rex ten̄ in dn̄io *CHERCHEFELLE* . Eddid regina tenuit.
T̄c se defd̄ p̄ . xxxvii . hid̄ . 7 dim̄ . Modo ad op̄ regis
p̄ . xxxiiii . hid̄ . Tra . ē   In dn̄io sunt . iii . car̄ .

5 MERTON. Earl Harold held it. Then and now it answered
   for 20 hides. Land for 21 ploughs. In lordship 2 ploughs;
      56 villagers and 13 smallholders with 18 ploughs. A church.
      2 mills at 60s; meadow, 10 acres; woodland, 80 pigs.
   Value before 1066 £25; later £16; now £35; however, its holder
   pays £43.
      In Southwark 16 dwellings at 18s 2d belong to this manor.
      One Orcus holds 2 hides which always lay in (the lands of)
   this manor, but are in another Hundred. He held them himself
   before 1066. Then they answered for 2 hides, now for nothing.
   In lordship 1 plough. Meadow, 2 acres. Value always 20s.
      The Bishop of Lisieux holds 2 sulungs* in Kent which were
   attached to this manor before and after 1066, as the men of
   the Hundred testify. He claims as patron the Bishop of Bayeux;
   his reeve did not wish to enter a plea thereon.

   In WALLINGTON Hundred
6 WALLINGTON, in lordship. Before 1066 and now it answered
   for 11 hides. Land for 11 ploughs. In lordship 1 plough;
      15 villagers and 14 smallholders with 10 ploughs. 3 slaves.
      2 mills at 30s; meadow, 8 acres; woodland, which is in Kent.
      Richard of Tonbridge holds 1 virgate of this manor, with the
      woodland, whence he removed a countryman who dwelt there.
      Now it pays the Sheriff 10s a year.
   Value of the whole manor before 1066 £15; now £10.

   In REIGATE Hundred
7 REIGATE, in lordship. Queen Edith held it. Then it answered
   for 37½ hides, now for 34 hides, for the King's work.
   Land for .... In lordship 3 ploughs;

7 LXVII . uilti 7 XI . borđ . cū . XXVI . car̄ . Ibi . II . molini
de . XII . fot . iī . denar̄ min . 7 XII . ac p̄ti . Silua: CXL .
porc̄ . de pafnag . 7 de herbagio: XLIII . porc̄ .
Modo ap̄p̄ciat̄ . XL . liƀ . 7 tan̄t reddit .

Rex ten in dn̄io *CHINGESTVNE* . IN CHINGESTVN HD .
de firma regis . E . fuit . Tc̄ fe defđ p . XXXIX . hiđ . m̄ p nichilo .
Tra . e . XXX . II . car̄ . In dn̄io funt . II . car̄ . 7 q̄ter XX . 7 VI .
uilti 7 XIIII . borđ cū . XXV . car̄ . Ibi æccta . 7 II . ferui . 7 V .
molini đe . XX . fot . 7 II . pifcariæ de . X . fot . 7 tcia pifcaria
ualde bona . fed fine cenfu . Ibi . XL . ac p̄ti . Silua . VI . porc̄ .
T . R . E . 7 poft . 7 modo . ualuit . XXX . liƀ .
De uiltis huj uillæ habuit 7 ht̄ Hūfrid camerari unū
uillan̄ in cuftodia . caufa codunandi lanā reginæ .
De ipfo etiā accep̄ . XX . fot . in releuam̄ cū pat ej fuit mort .
IN COPEDEDORNE HD .
Rex ten in dn̄io *ETWELLE* . T . R . E . fe defđ p . XVI . hiđ
una v min . Modo p . XIII . hiđ 7 dim ad firmā . Tra . e
In dn̄io . e . I . car̄ . 7 XLVIII . uilti 7 IIII . borđ cū
XV . car̄ . Iƀi . II . molini de . X . fot . 7 XIIII . ac p̄ti . Silua:
de . C . porc̄ . De herbagio: XI . porc̄ .
T . R . E . ualeƀ . XX . liƀ . 7 poft: 7 m̄ XVI . liƀ . 7 tam̄ reddit
XXV . liƀ . Teftant̄ hōes de hunđ qđ de hoc M̄ fubtractæ
funt . II . hidæ 7 una v . quæ ibi fuer̄ T . R . E . fed p̄pofiti
accōmodauer̄ eas fuis amicis . 7 unā denā filuæ . 7 unā croftā .
Ad hoc M̄ adjacet æccta de Leret . cū XL . acris træ .
Vat . XX . fot . Osƀn de Ow tenet .

67 villagers and 11 smallholders with 26 ploughs.
2 mills at 12s, less 2d; meadow, 12 acres; woodland, 140
  pigs from pasturage; from grazing, 43 pigs.
Now it is assessed at £40 and pays as much.

In KINGSTON Hundred

8 KINGSTON, in lordship. It was in King Edward's revenue. Then it
answered for 39 hides, now for nothing. Land for 32 ploughs.
In lordship 2 ploughs;
  86 villagers and 14 smallholders with 25 ploughs. A church;
    2 slaves.
  5 mills at 20s; 2 fisheries at 10s; a third fishery, excellent,
    but without dues; meadow, 40 acres; woodland, 6 pigs.
Value before 1066, later and now £30.
  Of the villagers of this village, Humphrey the Chamberlain had
and has one villager in his charge for the collecting of the
Queen's wool. He also took 20s from him as in-going* when
his father died.

In COPTHORNE Hundred

9 EWELL, in lordship. Before 1066 it answered for 16 hides,
less 1 virgate; now for 13½ hides, to the revenue.
Land for .... In lordship 1 plough;
  48 villagers and 4 smallholders with 15 ploughs.
  2 mills at 10s; meadow, 14 acres; woodland at 100 pigs;
    from grazing, 11 pigs.
Value before 1066, £20; later and now £16; however, it pays £25.
  The men of the Hundred testify that 2 hides and 1 virgate*
were removed from this manor; they were there before 1066,
but the reeves lent them to their friends; and 1 woodland
pig pasture and 1 croft.
  The church of Leatherhead is attached to this manor,
with 40 acres of land. Value 20s. Osbern of Eu holds it.

Rex ten in dnĩo *FECEHĀ*. Eddid regina tenuit. Tc̃ ſe defđ p̃.VII. hiđ. modo p̃ nulla. Tra. ē̃   In dnĩo
ē dimĩd car? 7.III. uiłłi 7 x. borđ. cũ. II. car̃. Ibi. IIII. molini de. IIII. ſoł. 7 x. ac̃ p̃ti. De paſnag̃ 7 herbag̃. VI. porc̃.
T.R.E. 7 poſt. uałb. LX. ſoł. Modo. L. ſoł.

Rex ten in dnĩo *GOMESELLE*. Herald tenuit. Tc̃ ſe defđ p̃. xx. hiđ. modo p̃ nichilo. Tra. ē̃. xx. car̃. In dnĩo ſunt. II.
7 xxx. uiłłi 7 VIII. borđ cũ xVIII. car̃. Ibi. VI. ſerui. 7 uñ moliñ de. xL. deñ. 7 III. ac̃ p̃ti. Silua. de xxx. porc̃.
T.R.E. uałb. xv. lib. 7 poſt. x. lib. Modo. xx. lib. 7 tam̃ redđ. xxx. lib. Huj̃ uillæ uillani. ab oñi re uicecom̃ ſt̃ đcti.
De tra huj̃ m̃ poſuit eps̃ dim̃ hidā in m̃ Brunlei in juſte. 7 eā tenet. quæ fuerat T.R.E 7 etiā W. in Gomeſelle.
In *WODETONE* hđ ht̃ rex in dnĩo. I. hiđ. quæ jacet in Gomeſelle.

Rex ten in dnĩo *SIRA*. Eddid regina tenuit.
Tc̃ ſe defđ p̃. IX. hiđ 7 tam̃ erant tc̃ ibi. xVI. hidæ. Modo ñ deđ geld̃. Tra. ē̃. xIIII. car̃. In dnĩo ſunt. II. car̃. 7 xIx.
uiłłi 7 VI. borđ cũ. XII. car̃. Ibi æccła 7 VI. ſerui. 7 II. molini de. x. ſoł. 7 III. ac̃ p̃ti. Silua. de. L. porc̃.
T.R.E. 7 poſt. 7 m̃. ual. xv. lib.   F 7 ibi ſuɴ app̃ciatæ.
In *WODETONE* hunđ ht̃ rex in dnĩo. III. virg̃. quæ jac̃ in Effire.

Rex ten in dnĩo *DORCHINGES*. Eddid regina tenuit. Tc̃ ſe defđ p̃. x. hiđ 7 dim̃. Modo p̃ nichilo. Tra. ē̃. xIIII. car̃. In dnĩo ſunt. II. car̃. 7 xxxVIII. uiłłi 7 XIII. borđ cũ. xIIII. car̃.
Ibi æccła. 7 IIII. ſerui. 7 III. molini de xv. ſoł 7 IIII. denar̃.
Ibi. III. ac̃ p̃ti. Silua. L. porc̃ de paſnag̃. De herbag̃. xxxVIII.
L̃ porc̃.

10 FETCHAM, in lordship. Queen Edith held it. Then it answered
for 7 hides, now for none. Land for .... In lordship ½ plough
and 2 oxen.
3 villagers and 10 smallholders with 2 ploughs.
4 mills at 4s; meadow, 10 acres; from pasturage and
grazing, 6 pigs.
Value before 1066 and later 60s; now 50s.

In BLACKHEATH Hundred
11 GOMSHALL, in lordship. Earl Harold held it. Then it answered
for 20 hides, now for nothing. Land for 20 ploughs. In lordship 2;
30 villagers and 8 smallholders with 18 ploughs. 6 slaves.
A mill at 40d; meadow, 3 acres; woodland at 30 pigs.
Value before 1066 £15; later £10; now £20; however, it pays £30.
The villagers of this village are exempt from all the
Sheriff's concerns.
The Bishop (of Bayeux) wrongfully placed ½ hide of the land
of this manor in the manor of Bramley, and holds it; it was in
Gomshall before and also after 1066.
In Wotton Hundred the King has 1 hide in lordship which lies in
(the lands of) Gomshall.

12 SHERE, in lordship. Queen Edith held it. Then it answered
for 9 hides; however, there were then 16 hides there. Now it
does not pay tax. Land for 14 ploughs. In lordship 2 ploughs;
19 villagers and 6 smallholders with 12 ploughs.
A church; 6 slaves.
2 mills at 10s; meadow, 3 acres; woodland at 50 pigs.
Value before 1066, later and now £15.
In Wotton Hundred the King has 3 virgates in lordship which
lie in (the lands of) Shere and are assessed there.

In WOTTON Hundred
13 DORKING, in lordship. Queen Edith held it. Then it answered
for 10½ hides, now for nothing. Land for 14 ploughs. In
lordship 2 ploughs;
38 villagers and 13 smallholders with 14 ploughs.
A church; 4 slaves.
3 mills at 15s 4d; meadow, 3 acres;
woodland, 50 pigs from pasturage; from grazing, 38 pigs.

T.R.E. 7 poſt . 7 modo. ual . xviii . lib.

Quidā Edric qui hoc Ⓜ tenuit ded . ii . hidas filiab͛ ſuis . 7 pö
tuer̄ ire quo uoluer̄ cū tris ſuis . Ex his hid h̄t Ricard de tone
brige unā . quæ nulli Ⓜ ptin . 7 ibi h̄t in dñio . i . car cū . i . bord
7 uñ moliñ ad hallā . 7 una a͞c p̄ti . Aliā hidā ten Herfrid de
cp̄o baioc . Ricardi hida. xx . ſol . Herfridi. x . ſol ualet.

De trib͛ Ⓜ quæ habuit regina Eddid in Sudrie. habet uice
comes . vii . lib . eo qd impendit eis adjutoriū cū op̄ habent.

IN GODELMINGE HVND.

Rex ten in dñio GODELMINGE . Rex . E . tenuit . T͞c . xxiiii . hidæ.
nunq̨ geldū reddid . Tra . ē . xxx . car . In dñio ſunt . iii . car . 7 L.
uilli . 7 xxix . bord cū . xix . car . Ibi . ii . ſerui . 7 iii . molini de . xli.
ſolid 7 viii . den . 7 xxv . a͞c p̄ti . Silua. c . porc.

T.R.E. ualb . xxv . lib . 7 poſt. xx . lib . Modo. xxx . lib ad numer.
7 tam̄ reddi ad penſū 7 arſurā . xxx . lib.

flanbard
ʄ Rannulf ten de hoc Ⓜ æcclam . cui ptin . iii . hidæ . Vlinær
tenuit de rege . E . Nunq̨ geld reddid . Tra . ē . ii . car . In dñio . ē una.
7 v . uilli 7 xii . cot cū . ii . car . Ibi xv . a͞c p̄ti . 7 Silua de . iii . porc.

Ibidē ten iſdē Rannulf alterā æcclam quæ redd . xii . ſol p anñ.
Hæ . iii . hidæ . T.R.E. 7 m̄. ual . iiii . lib . Cū recep. iii . lib.

Iſdē Rannulf ten de rege TIWESLE . Ad Godelminge ptinuit.
Leuuin tenuit de rege . E . T͞c 7 m̄ una hida . Ñ geld . Tra . ē . i . car.
7 ibi . ē cū uno uillo 7 vi . cot 7 uno ſeruo.

T.R.E. ualb . lx . ſol . 7 poſt . 7 m̄. xl . ſol.

IN AMELEBRIGE ten Aldi q̄dā femina de rege unā v . Val . iii . ſol.

Value before 1066, later and now £18.

   One Edric, who held this manor, gave 2 hides to his daughters, who could go where they would with their lands.

   Of these hides, Richard of Tonbridge has one, which belongs to no manor; he has 1 plough there in lordship with 1 smallholder, and a mill at the Hall; meadow, 1 acre.
Herfrid holds another hide from the Bishop of Bayeux.
Value of Richard's hide, 20s; of Herfrid's, 10s.

   From the three* manors which Queen Edith had in Surrey, the Sheriff has £7, because he aids them when they have work.

In GODALMING Hundred

14 GODALMING, in lordship. King Edward held it. Then 24 hides; they never paid tax. Land for 30 ploughs. In lordship 3 ploughs;
   50 villagers and 29 smallholders with 19 ploughs. 2 slaves.
   3 mills at 41s 8d; meadow, 25 acres; woodland, 100 pigs.
Value before 1066 £25; later £20; now £30 at face value; however, it pays £30, weighed and assayed.
   Ranulf Flambard holds the church of this manor, to which 3 hides belong. Wulfmer held it from King Edward; it never paid tax.
Land for 2 ploughs. In lordship 1;
   5 villagers and 12 cottagers with 2 ploughs.
   Meadow, 15 acres; woodland at 3 pigs.
Ranulf also holds a second church there, which pays 12s a year.
Value of these 3 hides before 1066 and now £4; when acquired £3.

15 Ranulf also holds TUESLEY from the King. It belonged to Godalming. Leofwin held it from King Edward. Then and now 1 hide; it did not pay tax. Land for 1 plough. It is there, with
   1 villager, 6 cottagers and 1 slave.
Value before 1066, 60s; later and now 40s.

In ELMBRIDGE [Hundred]

16 Aldith, a woman, holds 1 virgate from the King. Value 3s.

II. ARCHIEPS Lanfranc ten in dnio *CROINDENE* . T.R.E. se
defd p quat xx . hid . 7 modo p . xvi . hid 7 una v . Tra . e
.xx . car . In dnio sunt . iiii . car . 7 xlviii . uilli 7 xxv . bord . cu
.xxxiiii . car . Ibi æccla . 7 un molin de . v . sol . 7 viii . ac pti . Silua:
de . cc . porc.

De tra huj co ten Restold vii . hid de archiepo . Radulf . i . hida.
7 inde hnt . vii . lib 7 viii . sol . de gablo.

Totu T.R.E 7 post. ual . xii . lib . Modo: xxvii . lib archiepo.

Hominib3 ej. x . lib 7 x . solid.

Ipse archieps ten *CEIHA* de uictu monacho3 . T.R.E. se defd
p . xx . hid . 7 m p . iiii . hid . Tra . e . xiiii . car . In dnio sunt . ii . car.
7 xxv . uilli 7 xii . cot . cu . xv . car . Ibi æccla 7 v . serui . 7 una
ac pti . Silua: de . xxv . porc.

T.R.E. 7 post. ualuit . viii . lib . Modo: xiiii . lib . *IN BRIXIESTAN HD.*

Ipse Archieps ten in dnio *MORTELAGE* . T.R.E. se defd p quat xx.
hid . Canonici S Pauli ten de his . viii . hidas . quæ cu his gel
dauer 7 geldas . Modo geld simul p . xxv . hid . Tra . e . xxxv.
car . In dnio sunt . v . car . 7 quat . xx . uilli 7 xiiii . bord cu . xxviii.
car . Ibi æccla . 7 xvi . serui . 7 ii . molini de . c . solid . 7 xx . ac pti.
De silua: lv . porc de pasnag.

In Lundonia fuer . xvii . mansuræ reddent . lii . den . In Sud
werca: iiii . masuræ de xxvii . den . 7 de uilla putelei: xx . sol
de theloneo . 7 una piscaria sine censu . Hanc piscaria habuit

31 a Herald in Mortelaga T . R . E . 7 Stigand arch habuit diu . T . R . W .
7 tam dnt qd Herald ui construxit ea . T . R . E . in tra de Chin
gestune . 7 in tra S Pauli.

Tot co T . R . E . ualb xxxii . lib . 7 post: x . lib . Modo: xxxviii . lib.

2   LAND OF THE ARCHBISHOP OF CANTERBURY

In WALLINGTON Hundred

1 Archbishop Lanfranc holds CROYDON in lordship. Before 1066 it
answered for 80 hides; now for 16 hides and 1 virgate.
Land for 20 ploughs. In lordship 4 ploughs;
    48 villagers and 25 smallholders with 34 ploughs. A church.
A mill at 5s; meadow, 8 acres; woodland at 200 pigs.
    Restald holds 7 hides of the land of this manor from the
Archbishop; Ralph, 1 hide. They have £7 8s in tribute from it.
Total value before 1066 and later £12; now £27 to the
Archbishop, to his men £10 10s.

2 The Archbishop holds CHEAM himself, for the supplies of the monks.
Before 1066 it answered for 20 hides; now for 4 hides.
Land for 14 ploughs. In lordship 2 ploughs;
    25 villagers and 12 cottagers with 15 ploughs.
    A church; 5 slaves.
Meadow, 1 acre; woodland at 25 pigs.
Value before 1066 and later £8; now £14.

In BRIXTON Hundred

3 The Archbishop holds MORTLAKE himself, in lordship. Before 1066
it answered for 80 hides. The Canons of St. Paul's hold 8 of
these hides,* which paid and pay tax with these. Now they pay tax
together for 25 hides. Land for 35 ploughs. In lordship 5 ploughs;
    80 villagers and 14 smallholders with 28 ploughs.
    A church; 16 slaves.
    2 mills at 100s; meadow, 20 acres; from the woodland, 55 pigs
    from pasturage.
    In London there were 17 dwellings which paid 52d; in Southwark
4 dwellings at 27d; from the village of Putney 20s from tolls.
    1 fishery without dues. Before 1066 Earl Harold had this fishery   31a
in Mortlake. Archbishop Stigand had it for a long while after 1066.
However [the jurors] state that Harold established it by force
before 1066 on Kingston land, and on St. Paul's land.
Value of the whole manor before 1066 £32; later £10; now £38.

Bainiard ten de archiepo *WALEORDE* . T.R.E. fuit de ueſtitu
monachoʒ . Tc ſe defd p . v . hid . M p . iii . hid 7 dimid.
Tra . e . iii . car . In dnio . e una car . 7 xiiii . uilli 7 v . bord
cu . iii . car . Ibi æccla 7 viii . ac pti.

T.R.E. ualb . xxx . ſolid . 7 poſt. xx . ſol . Modo. lx . ſol.

Ipſe archieps ten *MERSTAN* *IN CHERCEFELLE HD.*
de ueſtitu monachoʒ . T.R.E. ſe defd p . xx . hid . Modo
p . v . hid . Tra . e . viii . car . In dnio ſunt . ii . car . 7 xxi.
uilts 7 iiii . bord cu . viii . car . Ibi æccla . 7 un molin de . xxx
denar . 7 viii . ſerui . 7 viii . ac pti . Silua. de . xxv . porc.
De herbagio. xvi . porc.

T.R.E. ualb . viii . lib . 7 poſt. iiii . lib . Modo. xii . lib.

Ipſe Archieps ten *HORSLEI* . *IN WOCHINGES HVND.*
de uictu monachoʒ . T.R.E. ſe defd p . xiiii . hid . Modo
p iii . hid . 7 una v 7 dim . Tra . e . v . car . In dnio . e una.
7 xiii . uilti 7 vi . bord . cu . vii . car 7 dimid . Ibi . iii . ſerui.
Silua. de . l . porc.   L redd . c . ſolid.
T.R.E. ualb . iiii . lib . 7 poſt . ſimilit . Modo. tntd . 7 tam

TERRA EPI WINTONIENSIS.

.III. Eps WINTONIENSIS ten *FERNEHAM* . *SCS PETRVS*
ſep tenuit . T.R.E. ſe defd p . lx . hid . 7 modo p . xl . hid.
Tra . e.   In dnio ſunt . v . car . 7 xxxvi . uilti 7 xi.
bord cu . xxix . car . Ibi . xi . ſerui . 7 vi . molini de xlvi . ſolid
7 iiii . denar . 7 xxxv . ac pti . Silua. de . cl . porc . 7 dim | paſnag.

4 Baynard holds WALWORTH from the Archbishop. Before 1066 it was
   for the clothing of the monks. Then it answered for 5 hides;
   now for 3½ hides. Land for 3 ploughs. In lordship 1 plough;
   14 villagers and 5 smallholders with 3 ploughs. A church.
   Meadow, 8 acres.
   Value before 1066, 30s; later 20s; now 60s.

In REIGATE Hundred

5 The Archbishop holds MERSTHAM himself, for the clothing of the
   monks. Before 1066 it answered for 20 hides; now for 5 hides.
   Land for 8 ploughs. In lordship 2 ploughs;
   21 villagers and 4 smallholders with 8 ploughs. A church.
   A mill at 30d; 8 slaves; meadow, 8 acres; woodland
      at 25 pigs; from grazing 16 pigs.
   Value before 1066 £8; later £4; now £12.

In WOKING Hundred

6 The Archbishop holds (East) HORSLEY himself, for the clothing of
   the monks. Before 1066 it answered for 14 hides; now for 3 hides
   and 1½ virgates. Land for 5 ploughs. In lordship 1;
   13 villagers and 6 smallholders with 7½ ploughs. 3 slaves.
   Woodland at 50 pigs.
   Value before 1066 £4; later the same; now as much; however,
   it pays 100s.

3   LAND OF THE BISHOP OF WINCHESTER

[In FARNHAM Hundred]

1 The Bishop of Winchester holds FARNHAM. St. Peter's (of Winchester)
   always held it. Before 1066 it answered for 60 hides; now
   for 40 hides. Land for .... In lordship 5 ploughs;
   36 villagers and 11 smallholders with 29 ploughs. 11 slaves.
   6 mills at 46s 4d; meadow, 35 acres; woodland at 150½ pigs
      for pasturage.

De tra huj m ten de epo Radulf . IIII . hid una v min.
Witts . III . hid . [7 unā uirg.] Wazo . dimid hid . In his tris . III . car in dnio.
7 XXII . uitti 7 IX . bord cū . VI . car . Silua: XXV . porc.
T.R.E. uatb m . LV . lib qd jacet in Sudrie . Qdo recep: XXX.
lib . Modo dniu epi: XXXVIII . lib . Hominū ej: IX . lib.
Æcctam huj m ten de epo Osbn de ow . Val . VI . lib . cū . I . hida
quā ht in Hantesira.

.II. TERRA OSBERNI EPI. *IN WOCHINGES HUND.*

.II. OSBERN eps ten *WOCHINGES* . Ipse tenuit T.R.E. 7 tc se
defd p . VIII . hid . Modo p . III . hid 7 dim . Tra . ē . IX . car 7 dim
In dnio una car 7 dim . 7 XX . uitti 7 VI . bord . cū . VIII . car 7 dim.
Ibi . III . serui . 7 uū molin de . XXX . denar . 7 XIIII . ac pti . Silua:
XXVIII . porc.

31 b Istud m habet 7 habuit ctuetudinē in silua regis de Wo
chinges . hoc . ē qd dns uillæ huj potest habe in ipsa silua
c.xx . porc sine pasnagio . Hoc m tenent . II . hoes de epo.
Ansgot 7 Godefrid . quisq . IIII . hid.
Totū . T.R.E. 7 post . ualuit . X . lib . Modo . IX . lib 7 X . sol.
Ipse eps ten *TETINGES* . Elmer [uenator] tenuit T.R.E. Tc se defd
p una hida . 7 m simit . Tra . ē . II . car . In dnio . ē una car.
7 un uitts 7 VI . bord cū . I . car . T.R.E. 7 post: [uat] III . lib . M: XL . sol.
Hoes de hund testant qd prestitū fuit [Istud m] p uicecomitē
ext firmā regis . E . 7 qd Osbn eps non habuit hoc m . T.R.E.

Ralph holds 4 hides, less 1 virgate of the land of this manor
from the Bishop; William, 3 hides and 1 virgate; Wace, ½ hide.
On these lands, 3 ploughs in lordship;
  22 villagers and 9 smallholders with 6 ploughs.
  Woodland, 25 pigs.
Value of the manor, of what lies in Surrey, before 1066 £55; when
acquired £30; now, the Bishop's lordship £38, his men's £9.
  Osbern of Eu holds the church of this manor from the Bishop.
Value £6, with 1 hide* which it has in Hampshire.

4   **LAND OF BISHOP OSBERN ***

In WOKING Hundred
1 Bishop Osbern holds WOKING. He held it himself before 1066.
Then it answered for 8 hides; now for 3½ hides.
Land for 9½ ploughs. In lordship 1½ ploughs;
  20 villagers and 6 smallholders with 8½ ploughs. 3 slaves.
  A mill at 30d; meadow, 14 acres; woodland, 28 pigs.
   This manor has and had a customary right in the King's woodland   31b
at Woking. That is why the lord of this village is able to
have 120 pigs without pasture dues in that woodland. Two men hold
this manor from the Bishop, Ansgot and Godfrey, 4 hides each.
Total value before 1066 and later £10; now £9 10s.

2 The Bishop holds TYTING himself. Aelmer Hunter held it before 1066.
Then it answered for 1 hide; now the same. Land for 2 ploughs.
In lordship 1 plough;
  1 villager and 6 smallholders with 1 plough.
Value before 1066 and later £3; now 40s.
  The men of the Hundred testify that this manor was leased through
the Sheriff outside King Edward's revenue and that Bishop Osbern
did not have this manor before 1066.

.V. Eps Baiocensis ten in dnio *BRVNLEI*. Alnod tenuit
de rege. E. Tc se defd ꝑ. xxxiiii. hid. Quattuor ex his
hid fuer liberoꝗ houm. qui de Alnod secede potuer.
Sup ħ. e tra ad. ii. car in ipso ꙳. quæ nunꝗ geld redd.
Modo oms istæ træ sunt in firma Brunlei. Tra. e. xxxv
car. In dnio sunt. vi. car. 7 qt xx 7 iiii. uilli 7 xl. cot
cu. xxxii. car. Ibi. iii. æcclæ. 7 xviii. serui. 7 v. molini
de. xxvi. sol. 7 xx. ac pti. Silua: de. c. porc.
T.R.E. ualb. xl. iol. 7 post: xxx. lib. Modo: lx. lib. 7 tam
redd qt xx. lib. xl. den min. Postꝗ eps saisiuit:
geldu non reddidit.

Ipse eps ten *CELEORDE*. In Brolege. Aluuin tenuit
7 potuit ire quo uoluit. Tc se defd ꝑ. iii. hid. modo pro
nichilo. Tra. e   In dnio. e una car. 7 vi. uilli 7 ii.
cot cu. ii. car. Ibi un molin de. vii. sol. Tot ual. lxx. sol.

Ϝ In Brunlege sunt adhuc. ii. hidæ. Anschil tenuit T.R.E.
7 potuit ire quo uoluit. Tc se defd ꝑ. ii. hid. m ꝓ nichilo.
Ibi. iii. uilli 7. i. cot cu. i. car. Tra. e. i. car. Val. xxxvi. sol.

Ϝ Ibide ht eps adhuc. ii. hid 7 dim. ꝗs Aluric tenuit
T.R.E. 7 cu eis potuit ire quo uoluit. Tra. e. ii. car. jacet
in Wodetone hund. Val. xxxii. sol.

Ϝ Isde eps ht ibi adhuc. i. hida. Quædā uidua ten. 7 T.R.E.
tenuit. 7 potuit ire quo uoluit. Tc se defd ꝑ una hida.
modo ꝓ nichilo. Val. x. sol.   *IN BLACHEFELDE. HVND.*

Ipse eps ht in dnio. iii. hid. Has tenuit Aluuard. 7 potuit
cu eis ire quo uoluit. Ibi sunt. v. uilli 7 viii. cot cu. ii. car.
Ibi. v. serui. 7 un molin de. xx. den. Tot ual ꝑ ann. c. sol.

5   LAND OF THE BISHOP OF BAYEUX

In BLACKHEATH Hundred

1a The Bishop of Bayeux holds BRAMLEY in lordship. Young Alnoth
held it from King Edward. Then it answered for 34 hides. 4
of these hides were free men's; they could withdraw from Alnoth.
Besides this there is land for 2 ploughs in this manor which never
paid tax. Now all these lands are in the Bramley revenue.
Land for 35 ploughs. In lordship 6 ploughs;
  84 villagers and 40 cottagers with 32 ploughs.
   3 churches; 18 slaves.
  5 mills at 26s; meadow, 20 acres; woodland at 100* pigs.
Value before 1066 £40;* later £30; now £60; however, it
pays £80 less 40d. Since the Bishop took possession it has not
paid tax.

1b The Bishop holds CHILWORTH himself. [It is] in Bramley. Alwin
Boy held it; he could go where he would. Then it answered for 3
hides; now for nothing. Land for .... In lordship 1 plough;
  6 villagers and 2 cottagers with 2 ploughs.
  A mill at 7s.
Total value 70s.

1c In Bramley there are 2 further hides.* Askell held them
before 1066; he could go where he would. Then it answered
for 2 hides; now for nothing.
  3 villagers and 1 cottager with 1 plough. Land for 1 plough.
Value 36s.

1d There the Bishop also has 2½ further hides, which Aelfric held
before 1066; he could go with them where he would.
Land for 2 ploughs. It lies in Wotton Hundred. Value 32s.

1e The Bishop also has 1 further hide there. A widow holds it and
held it before 1066; she could go where she would. Then it
answered for 1 hide; now for nothing. Value 10s.

In BLACKHEATH Hundred

1f The Bishop has 3 hides himself in lordship. Alfward held them;
he could go with them where he would.
  5 villagers and 8 cottagers with 2 ploughs. 5 slaves.
  A mill at 20d.
Total value 100s a year.

Ipſe eṗs h̅t in ipſo hund t̅r̅a ad . 1 . car̄ . Aluuin tenuit

T.R.E. Valet xxx . ſoł . T̅c̅   ſ recepit.

Tota t̅ra quæ ptiñ ad Brunlege . n̅ reddiđ gelđ poſtq eṗs

Ipſe eṗs ten in dñio *REDESSOLHA̅*. *IN GODELMINGE HD̅.*

Toui tenuit . T.R.E. 7 cū eo potuit ire quó uoluit . T̅c̅ ſe

defđ ꝑ . v . hiđ . Modo ꝑ nichilo . T̅ra . e̅ . 11 . car . Ibi ſunt

111 . uiłłi 7 1111 . cot̅ cū . 1 . car̅ . 7 11 . ᵃc̅ p̅ti . Silua:́ de 1111 . porc̅.

T.R.E. 7 poſt . 7 modo:́ uał . xl . ſoł.

Ipſe eṗs ten̅ in dñio *FERNECOME* . Anſgot tenuit . T.R.E.

7 cū eo potuit ire quó uoluit . T̅c̅ ſe defđ ꝑ . 111 . hiđ 7 dimiđ.

Modo ꝑ nichilo . T̅ra . e̅ . 11 . car . Ibi ſunt . v111 . uiłłi 7 111 . cot̅

31 c   cū . 11 . car̅ . 7 xv . ᵃc̅ p̅ti . Silua:́ 111 . porc̅ . Vał 7 ualuit . xx1111.

Quidā p̅poſit̅ regis n̅o̅e Lofus hoc M̅ calūniat̅ . 7 h̅o̅es

de Hund illi teſtificant̅ . q̇a tenebat illud de rege q̇do

fuit rex in Wales . 7 poſt tenuit . donec eṗs baioc̅ in Cheɴ preꝼ.

Ipſe eṗs c̅uertit ad firmā de Bronlei Reddeſolhā 7 Fernecome.

            IN TENRIGE HVND̅.

Anſchitill̅de Ros ten̅ de eṗo *TATELEFELLE* . Aluric te

nuit de rege . E . T̅c̅ 7 m̊ ſe defđ ꝑ dim̅ hida . T̅ra . e̅

In dñio . e̅ una car̅ . 7 v . uiłłi 7 1x . borđ cū . 1 . car̅ . Ibi . x11.

ſerui .   T.R.E:́ uałb . xxx . ſoł . 7 poſt:́ xl . Modo:́ lx.

Hugo ten̅ de eṗo un̅ M̅ qđ Cana tenuit de rege . E.

T̅c̅ ſe defđ ꝑ . 1111 . hiđ . m̊ ꝑ dim̅ . T̅ra . e̅ . 1111 . car̅ . In dñio

eſt una car̅ . 7 v . uiłłi 7 11 . borđ.

T.R.E. uałb . 1111 . lib̅ . 7 poſt:́ xx . ſoł . Modo:́ xl . ſoł.

1g The Bishop himself has land for 1 plough in this Hundred. Alwin held it before 1066. Value 30s. Then ....

1h All the land which belongs to Bramley has not paid tax since the Bishop acquired it.

In GODALMING Hundred

2 The Bishop holds RODSALL himself, in lordship. Tovi held it before 1066; he could go with it where he would. Then it answered for 5 hides; now for nothing. Land for 2 ploughs.
   3 villagers and 4 cottagers with 1 plough.
   Meadow, 2 acres; woodland at 4 pigs.
   Value before 1066, later and now 40s.

3 The Bishop holds FARNCOMBE himself, in lordship. Ansgot held it before 1066; he could go with it where he would. Then it answered for 3½ hides; now for nothing. Land for 2 ploughs.
   8 villagers and 3 cottagers with 2 ploughs.
   Meadow, 15 acres; woodland, 3 pigs.
   The value is and was 24s.
   A reeve of the King's named Lufa claims this manor. The men of the Hundred testify that he held it from the King, when the King was in Wales,* that he kept it afterwards until the Bishop of Bayeux came to Kent.* The Bishop himself transferred Rodsall and Farncombe to the Bramley revenue.

31c

In TANDRIDGE Hundred

4 Ansketel of Rots holds TATSFIELD from the Bishop. Aelfric held it from King Edward. Then and now it answered for ½ hide. Land for .... In lordship 1 plough;
   5 villagers and 9 smallholders with 1 plough. 12 slaves.
   Value before 1066, 30s; afterwards 40s; now 60s.

5 Hugh holds one manor from the Bishop, which Cana held from King Edward. Then it answered for 4 hides, now for ½.
   Land for 4 ploughs. In lordship 1 plough;
   5 villagers and 2 smallholders.
   Value before 1066, £4; afterwards 20s; now 40s.

Canonici baiocſes ten de epo *IN WALETONE HVND.*

MICHELHAM . ꝑ v . hiđ . Briſtric tenuit de rege . E.

Ipſe habuit . vi . hiđ | ſed unā ten Otƀt . quā Anteceſſor
dimidiam.
ej tenuit in uadio de Briſtrico ꝑ dim Marka auri.

In tra canonicoʒ ſunt . iiii . uilli 7 i . cot cū . ii . car . 7 uno
ſeruo . 7 xl . aͨ ꝑti . Tra . e . ii . car . Val 7 ualuit . xl . ſol.

In tra Otƀti ſunt . iiii . aͨ ꝑti . Val . vii . ſol . Nil āplius.

Anſgot ten dimid hiđ de epo . Val . v . ſol.

In ipſo ⹗ ten ipſi canonici de epo . ii . hiđ 7 dim . quas
duo hoͤs tenueꝛ de rege . E . Ibi . e in dͭnio . i . car . cū uno
uilło 7 ii . borđ . 7 i . ſeruo . 7 dim car . 7 xii . aͨ ꝑti . Sep . xx . ſol.

Ipſi canonici ten de epo *WITFORD* . Edmær tenuit
de rege . E . Tͨ 7 m̂ ſe deſđ ꝑ . iii . hiđ . Tra . e . ii . car . In
dͭnio . e una car . 7 ii . uilli 7 vi . cot . cū . ii . car . 7 ii . aͨ ꝑti.
T.R.E . 7 m̂ . ual . xxx . ſol . Cū recep⸝ x . ſol.

Ricard ten de epo *BENESTEDE* . Alnod tenuit de
rege . E . Tͨ ſe deſđ ꝑ . xxix . hiđ . modo ꝑ . ix . hiđ 7 dim.
Tra . e . xvi . car . In dͭnio ſunt . ii . car . 7 xxviii . uilli 7 xv.
cot . cū . xv . car . Ibi æccła 7 vii . ſerui . 7 uñ moliñ de . xx.
ſol . Silua⸝ de xx . porc . In Sudwerche . i . dom de . xl.
den ꝑtiñ huic ⹗ . 7 in Lundoñ una maſura dͭnica fuit
Alnod ꝑtiñ huic ⹗ . Nͨ ten Adā fili huƀti de epo.

Toͭ ⹗ T.R.E . ualƀ . x . liƀ . 7 poſt⸝ c . ſol . Modo⸝ viii . liƀ.
De tra huj ⹗ ten de Ricardo Goisfrid . v . hiđ . Radulf
ii . hiđ . Vlſi . ii . hiđ . Totū ual . vi . liƀ 7 . x . ſoliđ.

Iſđ Radulf ten de epo *SALVEDONE* . Derinc tenuit
de rege . E . Tͨ 7 m̂ ſe deſđ ꝑ . ii . hiđ . Tra . e . ii . car.
7 ibi ſunt in dͭnio . 7 una æccła.

T.R.E . ualƀ . xl . ſol . 7 poſt⸝ xx . ſol . Modo⸝ iiii . liƀ.

In WALLINGTON Hundred

6 The Canons of Bayeux hold MITCHAM from the Bishop for 5 hides.
Brictric held it from King Edward. He had 6½ hides himself,
but Odbert holds one, which his predecessor held in pledge from
Brictric for ½ gold mark.
On the Canons' land
4 villagers and 1 cottager with 2 ploughs and 1 slave.
Meadow, 40 acres. Land for 2 ploughs. The value was and is 40s.
On Odbert's land, meadow, 4 acres. Value 7s; nothing more.
Ansgot holds ½ hide from the Bishop. Value 5s.
In this manor the Canons hold 2½ hides themselves from the Bishop,
which 2 men held from King Edward. In lordship 1 plough, with
1 villager, 2 smallholders and 1 slave, and ½ plough.
Meadow, 12 acres.
(Value) always 20s.

7 The Canons hold WHITFORD* themselves from the Bishop. Edmer held
it from King Edward. Then and now it answered for 3 hides.
Land for 2 ploughs. In lordship 1 plough;
2 villagers, 6 cottagers with 2 ploughs.
Meadow, 4 acres.
Value before 1066 and now 30s; when acquired 10s.

8 Richard holds BANSTEAD from the Bishop. Alnoth held it from
King Edward. Then it answered for 29 hides, now for 9½ hides.
Land for 16 ploughs. In lordship, 2 ploughs;
28 villagers and 15 cottagers with 15 ploughs.
A church; 7 slaves.
A mill at 20s; woodland at 20 pigs.
In Southwark one house at 40d belongs to this manor. In London
one lord's dwelling, [which] was Alnoth's, belongs to this manor.
Now Adam son of Hubert holds it from the Bishop.
Value of the whole manor before 1066 £10; later 100s; now £8.
Geoffrey holds 5 hides of the land of this manor from Richard;
Ralph 2 hides; Wulfsi 2 hides; total value, £6 10s.

9 Ralph also holds CHALDON* from the Bishop. Dering held it from
King Edward. Then and now it answered for 2 hides. Land for 2
ploughs; they are there, in lordship. A church.
Value before 1066, 40s; later 20s; now £4.

E̅ps Lifoienfis ten de epo *IN BRIXISTAN HVND*.

HACHEHA̅. Brixi tenuit de rege . E . T̅c̅ 7 m̊ fe defd

p . III . hid . Tra . e̅ . III . car̅ . Ibi funt . IX . uilli 7 II . bord

cu̅ . III . car̅ . 7 ibi . VI . ac̅ p̊ti . Silua . III . porc̅.

T.R.E. 7 poft. 7 m̊ : ual . XL . folid . *IN CHIRCHEFELD HD̅*.

H̅erfrid ten de epo *GATONE* . Leuuin tenuit . T̅c̅ fe

defd p . X . hid . Modo p . II . hid 7 dimid . Tra . e̅ . V . car̅.

In d̅n̅io funt . II . car̅ . 7 VI . uilli 7 III . bord cu̅ . II . car̅ . Ibi æccła

7 VI . ac̅ p̊ti . Silua 7 herbagiu̅ : VII . porc̅.

T.R.E. 7 m̊ : ual . VI . lib̅ . Cu̅ recep : III . lib̅.

A̅nfgot ten de epo dim hid in Waletone hund . Hanc

tenuit Epi . T.R.E. 7 potuit ire quo uoluit . Val . V . folid.

E̅ps Lifoicenfis ten de epo *IN BRIXISTAN HVND̅*.

PECHEHA̅. Alfled tenuit de Heraldo T.R.E. 7 jacuit in pa

tricefy . T̅c̅ 7 m̊ fe defd p . II . hid . Tra . e̅ . I . car̅ . Ibi . e̅ un uilłs

7 III . bord . 7 II . ac̅ p̊ti . T.R.E. 7 m̊ : ual . XXX . fol . Cu̅ recep : XX . fol.

A̅nfgot ten de epo *ESTREHA̅* . Eduuin tenuit . T.R.E. 7 potuit

ire quo uoluit . T̅c̅ 7 m̊ fe defd p una hida . Ibi . e̅ . I . car̅ 7 II . uilli

Val 7 ualuit . XX.V. fol . *IN COPEDEDORNE HVND̅*.

H̅ugo ten de epo *PACHESHA̅* . Ælmer tenuit . T.R.E. de rege.

T̅c̅ fe defd p . IIII . hid . 7 m̊ p . III : uirg . Tra . e̅ . In d̅n̅io funt

. II . car̅ . 7 XI . uilli | cu̅ . II . car̅ . Ibi . IIII . ferui . 7 II . dimid molini

de XII . fol . 7 V . ac̅ p̊ti . Silua : III . porc̅.

T.R.E. ualb̅ . XL . fol . 7 poft : XX . fol . Modo : LXX . fol.

In BRIXTON Hundred

10 The Bishop of Lisieux holds HATCHAM from the Bishop. Brictsi
held it from King Edward. Then and now it answered for 3 hides.
Land for 3 ploughs.
9 villagers and 2 smallholders with 3 ploughs.
Meadow, 6 acres; woodland, 3 pigs.
Value before 1066, later and now 40s.

In REIGATE Hundred

11 Herfrid holds GATTON from the Bishop. Earl Leofwin held it.
Then it answered for 10 hides, now for 2½ hides.
Land for 5 ploughs. In lordship 2 ploughs;
6 villagers and 3 smallholders with 2 ploughs. A church.   31d
Meadow, 6 acres; woodland and grazing, 7 pigs.
Value before 1066 and now £6; when acquired £3.

12 Ansgot holds ½ hide in Wallington Hundred from the Bishop. Oepi
held this land before 1066; he could go where he would. Value 5s.

In BRIXTON Hundred*

13 The Bishop of Lisieux holds PECKHAM from the Bishop. Aelfled
held it from Harold before 1066. It lay in (the lands of) Battersea. *
Then and now it answered for 2 hides. Land for 1 plough.
1 villager and 3 smallholders.
Meadow, 2 acres.
Value before 1066 and now 30s; when acquired 20s.

14 Ansgot holds STREATHAM* from the Bishop. Edwin held it
before 1066; he could go where he would. Then and now
it answered for 1 hide. 1 plough there.
2 villagers.
The value is and was 25s.

In COPTHORNE Hundred

15 Hugh holds PACHEVESHAM from the Bishop. Aelmer held it
before 1066 from the King. Then it answered for 4 hides, now
for 3 virgates. Land for .... In lordship 2 ploughs;
11 villagers and 8 smallholders with 2 ploughs. 4 slaves.
2 half mills* at 12s; meadow, 5 acres; woodland, 3 pigs.
Value before 1066, 40s; later 20s; now 70s.

Rannulf⁹ ten̄ de ep̄o unā hidā 7 unā v̄ . Leuric tenuit de He

raldo libam . 7 quo uoluit ire potuit . Modo h̄ t̄ra ſe defđ ꝓ una v̄ .

Ibi . II . uiłłi hn̄t dim̄ car̄ . T . R . E.᷄ xx . ſoliđ . 7 poſt.᷄ xII . Modo.᷄ x . ſoł .

Baingiarđ ten̄ de ep̄o . I . hidā . Quā Elmer tenuit de Heraldo.

7 quó libet ire potuit . Tc̄ ꝓ una hida . m̄ ꝓ una v̄ ſe defđ . In dn̄io

ē una car̄ . cū uno borđ . 7 dimiđ molin̄ de . vI . ſoł .

T . R . E . uałƀ . xx . ſoł . 7 poſt.᷄ x . ſoł . Modo.᷄ xxIIII . ſoł .

In Waletone hunđ . h̄t Adā fili⁹ Huƀti . I . hiđ de ep̄o . quæ nunꝗ

geldū dedit.

Ipſe ep̄s ten̄ CODINTONE . Leuuin⁹ tenuit . Tc̄ ſe defđ ꝓ . xxx . hiđ .

De qƀƶ teneƀ com . xx̊ . hiđ . 7 x . hiđ teneƀ alodiarij uillæ . ꝗ̄ cū

ſuis t̄ris quó uoleƀ recede poterant . Modo de his . x . ten̄ ep̄s . vI .

cū alijs . xx . Hæ . xxvI . hidæ . ſe defđ m̄ ꝓ . v . hiđ . Hoc ten̄ ep̄s

ꝓ uno M̄ . Ilƀt ten̄ nc̄ de ep̄o has . xxvI . hiđ . Ipſe . xxII . hidas .

7 un̄⁹ hō ej̄ . IIII . hiđ . In dn̄io . ē . I . car̄ . 7 vII . uiłłi 7 Ix . borđ

cū . vI . car̄ . Ibi . IIII . ſerui . 7 un̄ molin̄ de . xL . den̄ .

De his hiđ ten̄ Radulf⁹ . IIII . hiđ . Vluuin . I . hiđ . 7 III . partes

uni hidæ ten̄ de rege . In dn̄io ē . I . car̄ . 7 IIII . uiłłi 7 IIII . borđ

cū una car̄ .

Tot̄ M̄ T . R . E . uałƀ xI . liƀ . 7 poſt.᷄ c . ſoł . Modo.᷄ Ix . liƀ 7 xII . ſoł .

De t̄ra huj̄⁹ M̄ ten̄ Reſtalđ⁹ . II . hiđ . s; in Waleton hunđ redđ ratiō .

STEDE ten̄ canonici de ep̄o baiocħ . Turgiſus tenuit de Heraldo.

Tc̄ ſe defđ ꝓ . Ix . hiđ . Modo ꝓ . III . hiđ 7 uną v̄ . T̄ra . ē

In dn̄io ſunt . II . car̄ . 7 xxxIII . uiłłi 7 xI . borđ cū . xIIII . car̄ .

Ibi . Ix . ſerui . 7 vII . porc̄ de herbagio . 7 IIII . ac̄ p̄ti .

T . R . E . uałƀ . x . liƀ . 7 poſt.᷄ vI . liƀ . Modo.᷄ xII . liƀ .

16 Ranulf holds 1 hide and 1 virgate from the Bishop. Leofric held
it free from Harold; he could go where he would. Now this land
answers for 1 virgate.
    2 villagers have ½ plough.
[Value] before 1066, 20s; later 12s; now 10s.

17 Baynard holds 1 hide from the Bishop, which Aelmer held from Earl
Harold; he could go where he would. Then it answered for 1
hide, now for 1 virgate. In lordship 1 plough, with
    1 smallholder.
    ½ mill at 6s.
Value before 1066, 20s; later 10s; now 24s.

18 In Wallington Hundred Adam son of Hubert has 1 hide from
the Bishop which never paid tax.

19 The Bishop holds CUDDINGTON himself. Earl Leofwin held it.
Then it answered for 30 hides, of which the Earl held 20 hides,
and the Freeholders of the village held 10 hides. They could withdraw
where they would with their lands. Now, of these 10 hides
the Bishop holds 6, with the 20 others. These 26 hides now answer for
5 hides. The Bishop holds them* as one manor.
Ilbert* now holds these 26 hides from the Bishop, 22 hides himself,
and one of his men 4 hides. In lordship 1 plough.
    7 villagers and 9 smallholders with 6 ploughs. 4 slaves.
    A mill at 40d.
Of these hides, Ralph holds 4 hides; Wulfwin holds 1 hide; and three
parts of 1 hide from the King. In lordship 1 plough;
    4 villagers and 4 smallholders with 1 plough.
Value of the whole manor before 1066 £11; later 100s; now £9 12s.
    Restald holds 2 hides of the land of this manor, but he
accounts for them in Wallington Hundred.

20 The Canons hold ASHTEAD from the Bishop of Bayeux. Thorgils held
it from Earl Harold. Then it answered for 9 hides, now for 3
hides and 1 virgate. Land for .... In lordship 2 ploughs;
    33 villagers and 11 smallholders with 14 ploughs. 9 slaves.
    From grazing, 7 pigs; meadow, 4 acres.
Value before 1066 £10; later £6; now £12.

Radulf⁹ ten de epo *TADEORDE* . Duo frs tenuer de rege . E.

7 quo uoluer ire potuer . Tc se defd ꝑ . v . hid . Modo ꝑ una hida

7 dimid . Tra . e . ii . car . In dnio una 7 dimid . 7 iii . uilli 7 iiii . bord

cu car 7 dimid . Ibi . i . seruus 7 i . porc de silua.

T . R . E . ualb . xl . sol . 7 post . 7 modo . xxx . solid.

Ricard⁹ ten de epo *FECEHA* . Biga tenuit de rege . E . Tc se

defd ꝑ . viii . hid | Modo ꝑ iiii . hid . Tra . e . v . car . In dnio . e una .

32 a 7 viii . uilli 7 iii . bord cu . i . car . Ibi . ii . serui . 7 v . pars

molini . 7 tcia pars alteri⁹ molini . 7 x . ac pti . 7 de pasnag

7 de herbag . xiii . porc . De molin . vi . sol 7 dimid.

T . R . E . 7 m . ual . lx . sol . Cu recep . l . solid.

Nigellus ten de epo *MICLEHAM* . Ansfrigus tenuit

de rege . E . Tc 7 m se defd ꝑ . v . hid . Tra . e . iiii . car . In

dnio sunt . ii . car . 7 iiii . uilli 7 iiii . bord 7 ii . serui . Ibi æccla.

7 ii . ac pti . Silua . de . iii . porc.

T . R . E . ualb . iii . lib . 7 post . l . sol . Modo . iiii . lib.

Hugo de port ten de epo *BERGE* . Tres libi hoes tenuer.

7 quo uoluer ire potuer . Tc se defd ꝑ . v . hid . Modo ꝑ . ii.

hid 7 dim . H . iiii . Maner ten Hugo ꝑ uno M . In Waleton

hund apꝑciatu . e.   *IN AMELEBRIGE HVND.*

Isde Hugo ten de epo . i . hida jn Aissela . 7 qda femina de eo.

Ibi . e un uilts . Val . v . sol . Qdo hugo hanc tra saisiuit.

non habuit inde libatore uel breue regis . sic hund testat.

Herfrid⁹ ten de epo *WEBRVGE* . duæ sorores tenuer . T . R . E.

7 quo uoluer cu tra se uertere potuer . Tc se defd ꝑ . iiii . hid.

modo ꝑ . ii . hid . Ibi . e un uilts . 7 i . bord . 7 xvi . ac pti . Silua.

de . v . porc . Val 7 ualuit . xl . sol . Qdo eps hanc tra saisi

uit . libatore l breue regis inde n habuer . sic Hund testat.

21 Ralph holds TADWORTH from the Bishop. Two brothers held it from
King Edward; they could go where they would. Then it answered
for 5 hides, now for 1½ hides. Land for 2 ploughs. In lordship 1½;
   3 villagers and 4 smallholders with 1½ ploughs. 1 slave.
   1 pig from the woodland.
Value before 1066, 40s; later and now 30s.

22 Richard holds FETCHAM from the Bishop. Bicga held it from
King Edward. Then it answered for 8½ hides, now for 4 hides.
Land for 5 ploughs. In lordship 1;
   8 villagers and 3 smallholders with 1 plough. 2 slaves.
   The sixth* part of a mill and the third part of another mill;
   meadow, 10 acres; from pasture and grazing, 13 pigs;
   from the mills, 6½s.
Value before 1066 and now 60s; when acquired 50s.

32a

23 Nigel holds MICKLEHAM from the Bishop. Ansfrid held it from
King Edward. Then and now it answered for 5 hides.
Land for 4 ploughs. In lordship 2 ploughs;
   4 villagers, 4 smallholders and 2 slaves. A church.
   Meadow, 2 acres; woodland at 3 pigs.
Value before 1066 £3; later 50s; now £4.

24 Hugh of Port holds BURGH from the Bishop. 3 free men held it;
they could go where they would. Then it answered for 5 hides,
now for 2½ hides. Hugh holds these 4 manors* as one manor.
It is assessed in Wallington Hundred.

  In ELMBRIDGE Hundred
25 Hugh also holds 1 free hide in ESHER from the Bishop,
and a woman from him.
   1 villager.
Value 5s.
   When Hugh took possession of this land, he did not have a
deliverer or the King's writ for it; so the Hundred testifies.

26 Herfrid holds WEYBRIDGE from the Bishop. Two sisters held it
before 1066; they could turn where they would with their land.
Then it answered for 4 hides, now for 2 hides.
   1 villager and 1 smallholder.
   Meadow, 16 acres; woodland at 5 pigs.
The value is and was 40s.
   When the Bishop took possession of this land, they* did not have
a deliverer or the King's writ for it; so the Hundred testifies.

Wadard ten de epo *DITONE.*   *IN CHINGESTVN HVND.*

Leuegar tenuit de Heraldo . 7 feruiebat ei . fƷ quo uoluiffet

cū tra ire potuiffet . Q̨do obijt: hanc trā tribƷ filijs fuis difpti

uit . T.R.E. Tc fe defđ ᵱ . vi . hiđ . modo ᵱ . ii . hiđ 7 dim . Tra . ē

ii . car . Ibi . ē car 7 dim . 7 iiii . borđ . 7 iiii . ferui . 7 pars molini

de . xv . den . 7 iiii . ac ᵱti . Silua: xx . porc.

T.R.E. uałb . iiii . lib . 7 poft: xl . fol . Modo: iiii . lib . Ille q̨ ten

de Wadardo: redđ ei . l . fol . 7 feruitiū uni militis.

Ipfe eᵱs hr in *SVDWERCHE* . uñ monafteriū 7 unū aque fluctū.

Rex . E . teneb die qua mortuus fuit . Qui æcclam habebat: de

rege tenebat . De exitu aquæ ubi naues applicabaɲ: rex habeb

ii . partes . Goduin tciā . Teftant u hoēs de hunđ franci 7 angli.

qđ eᵱs baioĉfis cū Rannulfo de his placitū inierit . fed ille

intelligens placitū ñ duci ᵱ rectitudinē ad ᵱficuū regis:

placitū deferuit . Eᵱs aut deđ æcclam 7 fluctū primū

Adeloldo . deinde Radulfo ᵱ excābio uni dom . Vicecomes

q̨qƷ negat fe ᵱceptū uel figillū regis de hac re unq̨ pcepiffe.

Hoēs de Suduuerca teftant . qđ T.R.E. null capieb thelo

neū in ftrande ł in uico Aquæ . nifi rex . 7 Siq̨s forisfaciens ibi

calūpniat fuiffet: regi emdabat . Si u non calūpniatus

abiffet fub eo qui facā 7 focā habuiffet: ille emdam | habet.

ᚠIpfi hoēs de Suduuerche deratiocinati fuɲ unā hagā 7 the

loneū ej ad firmā de Chingeftone . Hanc Euftachius teneb.

ᚠQđ rex hr in Suduuerche: apᵱciat . xvi . lib.

In Wodetone hunđ 7 in ō Sudtone habet eᵱs baioĉfis

ii . hiđ 7 dim . Herulf tenuit T.R.E. 7 q̨ uoluit ire potuit.

Tc fe defđ ᵱ . ii . hiđ 7 dim . modo ᵱ nichilo . Ħ apᵱciata 7 annu

merata funt in Brunlei ō eᵱi.

In KINGSTON Hundred

27 Wadard holds (Thames) DITTON from the Bishop. Leofgar held it
from Harold and served him, but he could go where he would with
the land. When he died, he divided this land between his
three sons, before 1066. Then it answered for 6 hides,
now for 2½ hides. Land for 2 ploughs. 1½ ploughs there;
  4 smallholders and 4 slaves.
    Part of a mill at 15d; meadow, 4 acres; woodland, 20 pigs.
  Value before 1066 £4; later 40s; now £4.
    Whoever holds it from Wadard pays him 50s, and the service of 1
man-at-arms.

[In BRIXTON Hundred]

28 In SOUTHWARK the Bishop has a monastery and a tidal waterway
  himself. King Edward held them at his death; whoever had the
  church held from the King. The King had two parts of the income
  from the waterway where ships moored, Earl Godwin the third part.
  But the men of the Hundred, French and English, testify that
  Bishop of Bayeux began a suit with Ranulf the Sheriff about them;
  but when he realised that the suit was not rightfully conducted to the
  King's advantage, he withdrew the suit. The Bishop however gave
  the church and the waterway first to Aethelwold, and then to Ralph,
  in exchange for a house. The Sheriff also denies that he ever
  received the King's command or seal in this matter.
    The men of Southwark testify that before 1066 no one but the
  King took toll on the shore or in the waterfront*.
  If a criminal was charged there, he paid his fine to the King;
  but if he was not charged, and went elsewhere, under a person who
  had full jurisdiction, that person had the culprit's fine.
    The men of Southwark were themselves adjudged one site
  and its tolls in the revenue of Kingston. Count Eustace held it.
  What the King has in Southwark is assessed at £16.

In WOTTON Hundred

29 and in the manor of SUTTON (-by-Shere) the Bishop of Bayeux has 2½
  hides. Herewulf held them before 1066; he could go where he would.
  Then it answered for 2½ hides, now for nothing.

30 These outliers* are assessed and enumerated in the Bishop's manor of
  Bramley.

TERRA ÆCCLÆ WESTMONAST IN BRICSISTAN HD.

.VI. Scs Petrvs de Weſtmonaſt. ten PATRICESŕ.

Herald tenuit. Tc ſe defd p̄. LXXII. hid. 7 m̄ p̄ XVIII. hid.

Tra. ē   In dñio ſunt. III. car. 7 XLV. uilli 7 XVI.

bord cū XIIII. car. Ibi. VIII. ſerui. 7 VII. molini de XLII.

lib 7 IX. ſol. 7 VIII. den. aut frūmtū ejdē p̄cii. 7 qt xx. 7 II.

ac p̄ti. 7 Silua: de. L. porc de paſnag. 7 In Sudwerche

.I. bord de. XII. den. De theloneo Wandeleſorde: VI. lib.

De uitto hn̄te. x. porc: uñ porc. Si min: nil dat.

De tra huj M̄ ten uñ miles. IIII. hid. Ej pecunia. cōputat

ſupius cū alia.   7 IX. ſol. 7 VIII. den.

Tot T.R.E. ualeb qter. xx. lib. 7 poſt: xxx. lib. Modo: LXXV. lib

Hoc M̄ ded rex. W. Sco petro. p̄ excābio de Windeſores.

De tra huj M̄ ten com moriton. I. hid 7 dimid. quæ

ibi erat. T.R.E. 7 poſt aliquādiu. Gifleb̄t p̄br. ten. III.

hid. eod m̄ fuerant. Eps Liſoienſis. II. hid. de qbȝ fuit

æccla ſaiſita T.R. Willi. 7 poſt deſaiſiuit eā eps baioc̄ſis.

Abb de Certeſi ten unā hid. quā p̄fect uillæ huj

p̄pt inimicitiā qdā ab iſto M̄ abſtulit. 7 miſit in Certeſi.

Ipſa abbatia de Weſtmonaſt ten IN WALETONE HD.

MORDONE. T.R.E. ſe defd p̄. XII. hid. Modo p̄. III. hid.

Tra. ē   In dñio ſunt. III. car. 7 VIII. uilli 7 V. cot

cū. IIII. car. Ibi uñ ſeruus. 7 uñ moliñ de. XL. ſolid.

T.R.E. ualb̄. VI. lib. Modo. x. lib. 7 tam redd. xv. lib.

Ipſa abbatia ten CLAIGATE. IN CHINGESTVN HD.

T.R.E. ſe defd p̄. II. hid 7 dim. m̄ p̄ dim hida. Tra. ē

II. car. In dñio eſt una. 7 III. uilli 7 II. bord. cū una car.

Ibi. V. ac p̄ti. Silua: de. I. porc. T.R.E. ualb̄. XL. ſol. Modo: L. ſol.

In BRIXTON Hundred
1 St. Peter's of Westminster holds BATTERSEA. Earl Harold held it.
   Then it answered for 72 hides, now for 18 hides. Land for ....
   In lordship 3 ploughs;
      45 villagers and 16 smallholders with 14 ploughs. 8 slaves.
      7 mills at £42 9s 8d, or corn of the same price; meadow, 82
   acres; woodland at 50 pigs from pasturage.
      In Southwark 1 smallholder at 12d; from the tolls of Wandsworth, £6;
   from a villager who has 10 pigs, 1 pig; if less, he pays nothing.
      1 man-at-arms holds 4 hides of the land of this manor; his stock
   is accounted above with the rest.
   Total value before 1066 £80; later £30; now £75 9s 8d.
      King William gave this manor to St. Peter's in exchange for Windsor.
   The Count of Mortain holds 1½ hides of the land of this manor;
   they were there before 1066 and for some time after.
      Gilbert the priest holds 3 hides; they were there in the same way.
   The Bishop of Lisieux, 2 hides of which the church had possession
   after 1066; but the Bishop of Bayeux dispossessed it later. *
      The Abbot of Chertsey holds 1 hide, which the reeve of this village
   took from the manor because of a feud, and put in Chertsey.

In WALLINGTON Hundred
2 The Abbey of Westminster holds MORDEN itself. Before 1066 it
   answered for 12 hides, now for 3 hides. Land for .... In
   lordship 3 ploughs;
      8 villagers and 5 cottagers with 4 ploughs. 1 slave.
      1 mill at 40s.
   Value before 1066 £6; now £10; however, it pays £15.

In KINGSTON Hundred
3 The Abbey holds CLAYGATE itself. Before 1066 it answered
   for 2½ hides, now for ½ hide. Land for 2 ploughs. In lordship 1;
      3 villagers and 2 smallholders with 1 plough.
      Meadow, 5 acres; woodland for 1 pig.
   Value before 1066, 40s; now 50s.

Ipſa abbatia teñ *TOTINGES*. IN BRICSISTAN HVND.

Suain tenuit de rege . E . 7 defd ſe ꝑ . IIII . hid . Tra . ē . I . car
7 dimid . Ibi ſunt . II . uilli cū dim car . 7 III . ac ꝑti .

T . R . E . 7 m̄ . ual . XL . ſol . Cū recep . XX . ſol .

Hanc trā acceꝑ Wallef de Suan . ꝑ morte regis . E .
7 inuadiauit ꝑ . II . mark auri Alnodo Lundonienſi .

Qui ꝯceſſit S petro ꝑ ſua anima . ſcilicet qd ibi habet .

Odbert teñ de S Petro . 7 nichil ded pro geldo .

Ipſa abbatia teñ *PELIFORDE*. IN GODELEI HVND.

Herald tenuit de rege . E . Antequā Herald habuiſſet .
defd ſe ꝑ . XXVII . hid . Poſtꝗ habuit . ꝑ XVI . hid ad libitū
heraldi . Hōes de hund nunꝗ audier nec uider breuē   Modo geld
ex parte regis qui ad tant poſuiſſet . Tra . XIII . car .   ꝑ . VIII . hid .

In dñio . ē una car . 7 XXXVII . uilli 7 XIIII . bord cū . VI . car .

Ibi . IIII . ſerui . 7 II . molini de . X . ſol . 7 XV . ac ꝑti . De paſ
nagio 7 herbagio . ꝗt XX . porc .

T . R . E . ualt . XII . lib . 7 poſt . X . lib . Modo . XVIII . lib .

De hac tra . ht rex . III . hidas in foreſta ſua .

TERRA SCI PETRI WINTON. IN WALETONE HVND.

VII ABBATIA SCI PETRI Winton teñ *SANDESTEDE*

T . R . E . ſe defd ꝑ . XVIII . hid . m̄ ꝑ . V . hid . Tra
ē . X . car . In dñio . ē una . 7 XXI . uilli 7 un cot cū . VIII . car .

32 c Ibi . IIII . ſerui . Silua . de . XXX . porc .
                                                                    lib.

T . R . E . ualt . C . ſol . 7 poſt . VII . lib . Modo . XII . lib . Tam redd . XV .

In BRIXTON Hundred

4 The Abbey holds TOOTING itself. Swein* held it from King Edward.
It answered for 4 hides. Land for 1½ ploughs.
2 villagers with ½ plough.
Meadow, 3 acres.
Value before 1066 and now 40s; when acquired 20s.
Earl Waltheof received this land from Swein after King Edward's
death. He pledged it for 2 gold marks to Alnoth of London,
who assigned it to St. Peter's for his soul's sake; that is,
what he had there. Odbert holds it from St. Peter's,
but has paid nothing in tax.

In GODLEY Hundred

5 The Abbey holds PYRFORD itself. Harold held it from King Edward.
Before Harold had it, it answered for 27 hides; after he had it,
for 16 hides, at Harold's will. The men of the Hundred have
never seen or heard of a writ on the King's behalf, which placed
it at such (an amount). Now it pays tax for 8 hides.
Land for 13 ploughs. In lordship 1 plough;
37 villagers and 14 smallholders with 6 ploughs. 3 slaves.
2 mills at 10s; meadow, 15 acres; from pasturage and
grazing, 80 pigs.
Value before 1066 £12; later £10; now £18.
The King has 3 hides of this land in his Forest.

7   LAND OF ST. PETER'S OF WINCHESTER

In WALLINGTON Hundred

1 The Abbey of St. Peter's of Winchester holds SANDERSTEAD.
Before 1066 it answered for 18 hides, now for 5 hides.
Land for 10 ploughs. In lordship 1;
21 villagers* and 1 cottager with 8 ploughs. 4 slaves.   32c
Woodland at 30 pigs.
Value before 1066, 100s; later £7; now £12; however, it pays £15.

.VIII. ABBATIA Sc̄I PETRI de CERTESẎ teñ *WATENDONE.*

T.R.E. ſe defđ ꝑ. xx. hiđ. Modo ꝑ. v. hiđ. Tra. e̅. viii. car.

In dn̄io. e̅ una car. 7 xvii. uiłłi 7 ii. cot cū. v. car. Ibi æccła.

Silua: vi. porc de paſnag. T.R.E. uałb. vi. lib. Modo: vii. lib.

Ipſa abbatia teñ *COLESDONE.* T.R.E. ſe defđ ꝑ. xx. hiđ.

Modo ꝑ. iii. hiđ 7 dim̄. Tra. e̅. x. car. In dn̄io. e̅ una car.

7 x. uiłłi 7 iiii. cot cū. vi. car. Ibi æccła. Silua: de. iii. porc.

T.R.E. uałb. vi. lib. Modo: vii. lib.

Ipſa abbatia teñ *SVDTONE.* T.R.E. ſe defđ ꝑ xxx. hiđ.

Modo ꝑ. viii. hiđ 7 dimiđ. Tra. e̅. xv. car. In dn̄io ſuɴ. ii. car.

7 xxi. uiłłs 7 iiii. cot cū. xiii. car. Ibi. ii. æcclæ. 7 ii. ſerui.

7 ii. ac̄ p̃ti. Silua: de. x. porc. T.R.E. uałb. xx. lib. M̄. xv. lib.

Ipſa abbatia teñ. ii. hiđ træ *IN TENRIGE HVND* In ipſo hđ teñ ipſa es abbatia. iii. uirg træ.

7 Wiłłs teñ de abbe. S; hoēs teſtant qđ fuit tra dn̄ica

Aluuini. T.R.E. 7 quo uoluit ire potuit.

Tc̄ ſe defđ ꝑ. ii. hiđ. modo ꝑ nichilo. Ibi. e̅ uñ borđ. 7 uñ

ſeruus. T.R.E. uałb. xx. ſoł. 7 poſt: v. ſoł. Modo: x. ſoliđ.

Ipſa abbatia teñ *COVENHA.* *IN AMELEBRIGE HVND.*

T.R.E. ſe defđ ꝑ. xxx. hiđ. Modo ꝑ xii. hiđ 7 dimidia.

Tra. e̅. x. car. In dn̄io. e̅. i. car. 7 xxix. uiłłi 7 vi. cot cū

ix. car. Ibi. iii. molini de. xiii. ſoł 7 iiii. denar. 7 una ac̄

p̃ti. Silua: xl. porc. T.R.E. uałb. xx. lib. Modo: xiiii. lib.

LAND OF THE CHURCH OF CHERTSEY

In WALLINGTON Hundred
1 The Abbey of St. Peter's of Chertsey holds WADDINGTON.
Before 1066 it answered for 20 hides, now for 5 hides.
Land for 8 ploughs. In lordship 1 plough.
  17 villagers and 2 cottagers with 5 ploughs. A church.
  Woodland, 6 pigs from pasturage.
Value before 1066 £6; now £7.

2 The Abbey holds COULSDON itself. Before 1066 it answered for 20 hides,
now for 3½ hides. Land for 10 ploughs. In lordship 1 plough;
  10 villagers and 4 cottagers with 6 ploughs. A church.
  Woodland for 3 pigs.
Value before 1066 £6; now £7.

3 The Abbey holds SUTTON (-by-Cheam) itself. Before 1066 it
answered for 30 hides, now for 8½ hides. Land for 15 ploughs.
In lordship 2 ploughs;
  21 villagers* and 4 cottagers with 13 ploughs.
  2 churches; 2 slaves.
  Meadow, 2 acres; woodland at 10 pigs.
Value before 1066 £20; now £15.

In TANDRIDGE Hundred
4 The Abbey holds 2 hides of land itself and William holds them from
the Abbot, but the men (of the Hundred) testify that it was Alwin's
lord's land before 1066 and that he could go where he would.
Then it answered for 2 hides, now for nothing.
  1 smallholder and 1 slave.
Value before 1066, 20s; later 5s; now 10s.

5 In this Hundred the Abbey holds 3 virgates of land itself.*

In ELMBRIDGE Hundred
6 The Abbey holds COBHAM itself. Before 1066 it answered for 30 hides,
now for 12½ hides. Land for 10 ploughs. In lordship 1 plough;
  29 villagers and 6 cottagers with 9 ploughs.
  3 mills at 13s 4d; meadow, 1 acre; woodland, 40 pigs.
Value before 1066 £20; now £14.

Witts de Wateuile ten̾ . 11 . hiđ de ipſa abbatia.

Vn̾ anglic̾ tenuit T.R.E. 7 ipſo rege uiuente deđ hanc tra̅ eiđ æcclæ in elemoſina . Ħ tra̅ . ē de ꝏ Aiſſele.

Ibi ſunt . vi . uiłłi cū̄ . 11 . car̾ . T.R.E. 7 m̾.̔uał x111i . ſoł 7 vi.den̾.

In̾ eađ uilla Aiſſela hɫ Iſđē Witts de abbatia Certeſẏ ſic̄ dic̄ . 111 . hiđ 7 dimiđ . T.R.E. tenueꝵ un̾ hō 7 11 . femi næ . 7 quo uolueꝵ ſe uertere potueꝵ . ſ; ꝓ defenſione ſe cū̄ tra abbatiæ ſūmiſeꝵ . Ibi ſunt . 11 . uiłłi cū̄ . 1 . car̾.

T.R.E. uałb . xvi . ſoł . 7 poſt.̔v . ſoł . Modo.̔x . ſoł.

Hæ . v . hidæ 7 dimiđ . ſuꝑđictæ. ſe defđt ꝓ . v . uirg̾.

Ipſa abbatia ten̾ EVESHĀ IN COPEDORNE HVNĐ.

T.R.E. ſe defđ ꝓ . xxx111i . hiđ . Modo ꝓ . x1 . hiđ.

Tra . ē . xv11 . car̾. In dn̅io . ē una . 7 xxx111i . uiłłi 7 1111.

borđ cū̄ . xv11 . car̾. Ibi . 11 . æcclæ 7 vi . ſerui . 7 11 . mo lini de . x . ſoliđ . 7 xx111i . ac̄ p̄ti . Silua.̔ de . xx . porc̄.

T.R.E. uałb . xx . lib̄ . Modo.̔xv11 . lib̄.

In WEBRIGE hacten̾ tenuit

ipſa abbatia . 11 . hiđ . Alured tenuit T.R.E. 7 poſt morte̅ ej . 7 quolibet ſe uertere potuit . Tc̄ 7 m̾ . 11 . hiđ.

Ibi ſunt . 111 . uiłłi . 7 v111 . ac̄ p̄ti . Silua . 11 . porc̄ . Sep̄

In eađ uilla hɫ un̾ anglic̾ . 11 . hiđ de   ƒ xx . ſoł.

ipſa abbatia . Ipſe tenuit T.R.E. 7 cū̄ ea quo uoluit ſe uertere potuit . Ibi . ē una car̾ . 7 11 . uiłłi cū̄ dim̾ car̾ . 7 v111 . ac̄ p̄ti . Silua.̔11 . porc̄ . Vał ⁊ ualuit . xx . ſoł.

7 William of Watteville holds 2 hides from the Abbey itself. An
   Englishman held them before 1066, and in King Edward's lifetime
   he gave this land to this church in alms. The land is the manor of Esher's.
   6 villagers with 2 ploughs.
   Value before 1066 and now 14s 6d.

8 In the same village, ESHER, William also has 3½ hides from the Abbey
   of Chertsey, as he says. Before 1066 1 man and 2 women
   held them; they could turn where they would, but for their
   protection they put themselves under the Abbey with the land.
   2 villagers with 1 plough.
   Value before 1066, 16s; later 5s; now 10s.
   The above 5½ hides answer for 5 virgates.

In COPTHORNE Hundred
9 The Abbey holds EPSOM itself. Before 1066 it answered for 34
   hides, now for 11 hides. Land for 17 ploughs. In lordship 1;
   34 villagers and 4 smallholders with 17 ploughs.
   2 churches; 6 slaves.
   2 mills at 10s; meadow, 24 acres; woodland at 20 pigs.
   Value before 1066 £20; now £17.

[In ELMBRIDGE Hundred]
10 In WEYBRIDGE the Abbey has hitherto held 2 hides itself. Alfred
   held them before 1066 and later. He could turn wherever
   he would. Then and now 2 hides.
   3 villagers.
   Meadow, 8 acres; woodland, 2 pigs.
   [Value] always 20s.

11 In the same village an Englishman has 2 hides from the Abbey itself.
   He held them himself before 1066 and could turn with the (land)
   where he would. 1 plough there.
   2 villagers with ½ plough.
   Meadow, 8 acres; woodland, 2 pigs.
   The value is and was 20s.

Edricus teñ de ipſa abbatia dim̃ hidã. *IN CHINGESTUN HD̄.*

quã p . ii . annos ante mortē R . E . abbatia tenuit . Antea teneb̃

iii . hões de ipſo rege . ſ; ñ poterañ recede ſire p̃cepto regis.

q̃a bedelli erant in Chingeſtone . Tc̃ 7 m̃ ſe deſđ p̃ dim̃ hida.

Tra . e . iii . boũ . Ibi ſunt . vii . boues . cũ . i . borđ . 7 ii . ãc p̃ti.

T . R . E . ualb̃ . vii . ſoł . modo . viii . ſoł.

Wiłłs de Wateuile teñ *MELDONE* de feuo abbis . Abb̃ te

nuit T . R . E . Tc̃ ſe deſđ p̃ . ii . hiđ . m̃ p̃ una hida . una v̄ miñ.

Tra . e . i . car . Ibi ſunt . iiii . uiłłi cũ dim̃ car . Vał 7 ualuit . xx . ſoł.

Ipſa abbatia teñ in dñio *PATRICESHA* . T . R . E . ſe deſđ p̃ . x.

hiđ . m̃ p̃ . iiii . hiđ . Tra . e . v . car . In dñio . e una car . 7 xv . uiłłi

7 ii . borđ . cũ . iiii . car . Ibi æccła . 7 piſcar de mille anguiłł.

7 mille Lãpriduł . 7 iii . ãc p̃ti . T . R . E . ual . c . ſoł . M̃ . vi . lib̃ 7 x . ſoł.

Haimo uicecom teñ *ESTREHA* de ipſa abbatia . Vluuarđ

tenuit de rege . E . 7 quo uoluit ire potuit . Tc̃ ſe deſđ p̃ una hida.

Tra . e . i . car . Ibi ſunt . ii . borđ .   Vał 7 ualuit . xx . ſoł.

Rainalđ teñ unã hiđ jn Aiſſela . *IN AMELEBRIGE HVND̄.*

de ipſa abbatia . 7 p̃ xv . acris deđ gelđ . Quædã femina tenuit T . R . E.

7 potuit ire quo uoluit . ſ; p̃ defenſione ſub abbatia ſe miſit . Ibi ſunt . iii.

Ipſa abbatia teñ *BOCHEHA IN FINGEHA HVND̄.* uiłłi . Vał . vii . ſoł.

T . R . E . ſe deſđ p̃ . xx hiđ . 7 m̃ p̃ . xiii . hiđ . Tra . e . xix . car . In

dñio . e una car . 7 xxxii . uiłłi 7 iiii . borđ cũ . xviii . car . Ibi æccła

7 iii . ſerui . 7 uñ moliñ de . x . ſoł . 7 vi . ãc p̃ti . Silua . de quať xx.

In KINGSTON Hundred

12 Edric holds ½ hide from the Abbey itself, which the Abbey held
for two years before 1066. Previously three men held it from the King
himself, but they could not withdraw without the King's command,
because they were beadles in Kingston. Then and now it answered
for ½ hide. Land for 3 oxen. 7 oxen there, with 1 smallholder.
  Meadow, 2 acres.
Value before 1066, 7s; now 8s.

13 William of Watteville holds MALDEN from the Abbot's holding. The
Abbot held it before 1066. Then it answered for 2 hides, now
for 1 hide less 1 virgate. Land for 1 plough.
  4 villagers with ½ plough.
The value is and was 20s.

14 The Abbey holds PETERSHAM itself, in lordship. Before 1066 it
answered for 10 hides, now for 4 hides. Land for 5 ploughs.
In lordship 1 plough;
  15 villagers and 2 smallholders with 4 ploughs. A church.
  A fishery at 1000 eels and 1000 lampreys; meadow, 3 acres.
Value before 1066, 100s; now £6 10s.

15 Hamo the Sheriff holds HAM* from the Abbey itself. Wulfward
held it from King Edward; he could go where he would.
Then it answered for 1 hide. Land for 1 plough.
  2 smallholders.
The value is and was 20s.

In ELMBRIDGE Hundred

16 Reginald holds 1 hide in ESHER from the Abbey itself. He gave
the tax for 15 acres. A woman held it before 1066; she could go
where she would, but for her protection she put herself under the Abbey.
  3 villagers.
Value 7s.

In EFFINGHAM Hundred

17 The Abbey holds (Great) BOOKHAM itself. Before 1066 it answered
for 26 hides, now for 13 hides. Land for 19 ploughs.
In lordship 1 plough.
  32 villagers and 4 smallholders with 18 ploughs.
  A church; 3 slaves.
  1 mill at 10s; meadow, 6 acres; woodland at 80 pigs;
  from grazing, 30 pigs.

porc̄. De herbagio:ˊxxx.porc̄. De hac t̄ra ten̄ Gunfrid̄.ɪ.hid̄.7 ibi
hī.ɪ.car̄.   Toī ꝏ T.R.E. ualb̄.xvɪ.lib̄.Modo:ˊxv.lib̄.
Ipſa abbatia jacet in GODELEI HVND̄.7 ipſa uilla T.R.E.7 m̄
ſe defd̄ ‿p.v.hid̄.Tra.ē   In dn̄io ſunt.ɪɪ.car̄.7 xxxɪx.
uiłłi 7 xx.bord̄ cū.xvɪɪ.car̄. Ibi uñ moliñ ad hallā.7 cc.ac̄ p̄ti.
Silua.de.ʟ.porc̄ de paſnag.7 una ferraria quæ opat̄ ad hallā.
De his.v.hid̄ ten̄ Ricard̄.ɪɪ. hid̄ 7 dim̄.ſub rege W.Sed hund̄
teſtat̄ q̄d̄ anteceſſor ej̄ tenuit de abbatia.nec poterat alias ire ſine
abb̄is lic̄tia. Ibi hī in dn̄io.ɪ.car̄.7 uñ uiłł 7.ɪɪɪɪ.bord̄ cū.ɪ.car̄.
Toī ꝏ T.R.E.ualb̄.xvɪɪɪ.lib̄.Modo:ˊxxɪɪ.lib̄.Q̄d̄ Ricard̄ ten̄:ˊxʟ.ſoł.
Ipſa abbatia ten̄ TORP. In Godelei HVND̄.T.R.E.ſe defd̄ ‿p.x.hid̄.
modo ‿p.vɪɪ.hid̄.Tra.ē   In dn̄io.ē.ɪ.car̄.7 xxɪɪɪɪ.uiłłi 7 xɪɪ.
bord̄.cū.vɪɪɪ.car̄.Ibi xxxɪɪɪ.ac̄ p̄ti.De herbagio:ˊxxɪɪɪɪ.porc̄.
T.R.E.7 modo:ˊuał.xɪɪ.lib̄.   IN FINGEHĀ HVND̄.
Oſuuold̄ ten̄ de ipſa æccła EPINGEHA. Ipſemet tenuit T.R.E.
Tē ſe defd̄ ‿p vɪ.hid̄.modo ‿p.ɪɪ.hid̄ 7 dim̄.Ibi ſunt.ɪɪ.uiłłi.7 ɪx.bord̄.
cū dim̄ car̄.7 una ac̄ p̄ti.7 de ſilua:ˊx.porc̄.de paſnag.Vał 7 ualuit.xʟ.ſoł.
Ipſa abbatia ten̄ EGEHA.T.R.E.ſe defd̄ IN GODELEI HVND̄.
‿p xʟ.hid̄.Modo ‿p xv.hid̄.Tra.ē xʟ.car̄.In dn̄io ſunt.ɪɪ.car̄.
7 xxv.uiłłi 7 xxxɪɪ.bord̄.cū.x.car̄.Ibi.cxx.ac̄ p̄ti.Silua.ʟ.porc̄
de paſnag.De herbag:ˊxxv.porc̄.T.R.E.ualb̄.xʟ.lib̄.M̄:ˊxxx.lib̄ 7 x.ſoł.
De hac t̄ra ten̄ Gozelin̄.ɪɪɪ.hidas.quæ T.R.E.fueī de dn̄io abbatiæ.

Gunfrid holds 1 hide of this land and has 1 plough there.
Value of the whole manor before 1066 £16; now £15.

In GODLEY Hundred*
18 lies the Abbey itself. Before 1066 and now the village
itself (CHERTSEY) answered for 5 hides. Land for ....
In lordship 2 ploughs;
   39 villagers and 20 smallholders with 17 ploughs.
   A mill at the Hall; meadow, 200 acres; woodland at 50 pigs
      from pasturage; a smithy which works for the Hall.
Of these 5 hides Richard Reckless* holds 2½ hides under King
William, but the Hundred testifies that his predecessor held from
the Abbey but could not go elsewhere without the Abbot's permission.
He has 1 plough there, in lordship;
   1 villager and 4 smallholders with 1 plough.
Value of the whole manor before 1066 £18; now £22;
what Richard holds 40s.

19 The Abbey holds THORPE itself, in GODLEY Hundred*. Before 1066 it
answered for 10 hides, now for 7 hides. Land for .... In
lordship 1 plough;
   24 villagers and 12 smallholders with 8 ploughs.
   Meadow, 33 acres; from grazing, 2´ pig.
Value before 1066 and now £12.

In EFFINGHAM Hundred
20 Oswald* holds EFFINGHAM from the Church itself. He held it himself
before 1066. Then it answered for 6 hides, now for 2½ hides.
Land for 2 ploughs.
   2 villagers and 9 smallholders with ½ plough.
   Meadow, 1 acre; from the woodland, 10 pigs from pasturage.
The value is and was 40s.

In GODLEY Hundred
21 The Abbey holds EGHAM itself. Before 1066 it answered for 40
hides, now for 15 hides. Land for 40 ploughs. In lordship 2 ploughs;
   25 villagers and 32 smallholders with 10 ploughs.
   Meadow, 120 acres; woodland, 50 pigs from pasturage;
      from grazing, 25 pigs.
Value before 1066 £40; now £30 10s.
   Jocelyn holds 3 hides of this land which were in the Abbey's
lordship before 1066.

Ipſa abbatia ten̄ *CEBEHA*.T.R E.7 m̄ ſe defđ ꝑ.x.hiđ.Tra.ē
xii.cař.In dn̄io.ē una.7 xxix.uiłłi 7 vi.borđ cū xi.cař.Ibi.iii.ſerui.
7 x.ãc ꝑti.Silua de.cxxx.porč.

De hac tra ten̄ Odm̄ de abb̄e.iiii.hiđ.Corbelin.ii.hiđ.de tra uiłłoꝣ.
In dn̄io.i.cař.7 vii.uiłłi 7 iiii.borđ cū.iii.cař.Ibi æccła ꝗ alia capella.

Totū m̄ T.R.E.uałb̄.xvi.lib̄.Modo pars monachoꝣ.xii.lib̄.
7 x.ſoliđ.Hõum û.́ lx.ſoliđ.

In *WALETONE HVND*.Haimo uicecomes ten̄ de abb̄e de Certeſỹ.i.hiđ
7 dim.in feudo.Aluuard tenuit T.R.E.7 potuit ſe uertere quo uoluit.
In dn̄io.ē una cař.cū.vi.cot.7 iii.ſeruis.7 xi.ãc ꝑti.T.R.E.7 poſt 7 modo.́
uał xx.ſoł.

Iſđē Hamo ten̄ dimiđ hidā de abbatia ipſa.Vluuard tenuit T.R.E.7 potuit
ſe uertere quo uoluit.Ibi un̄ cot.7 v.ãc ꝑti.Vał 7 ualuit.v.ſoł.
ᚠIſtæ.ii.hidæ ꝗs ten̄ haimo.T.R.E.ꝑ.ii.hiđ ſe defđ.m̄ ꝑ dimiđ.

IN *BRIXISTAN HVND*.Iſđē Haimo ten̄ *TOTINGES* de abb̄e de Certeſỹ.ꝑ
vi.hiđ ſe defđ una v' min'. T.R.E.Modo ꝑ nichilo.Tra.ē.iii.cař.In dn̄io.ē una cař
7 iii.uiłłi 7 ii.borđ.cū una cař.Ibi æccła.7 iiii.ãc ꝑti.T.R.E.
uałb̄ xl.ſoł.Poſt.́ xx.ſoliđ.Modo.́ lxx.ſoliđ.

Iſđē Haimo ten̄ in Totinges ūnā hidā de abb̄e de certeſỹ.Oſuuard tenuit de
rege.E.7 potuit ire quo uoluit.Ibi.ē uił uiłłs cū dimiđ cař.7 una ãc ꝑ
ᚠT.R.E.́ xv.ſoł.modo.́ x.ſoł.

22 The Abbey holds CHOBHAM itself. Before 1066 and now it answered
for 10 hides. Land for 12 ploughs. In lordship 1;
29 villagers and 6 smallholders with 11 ploughs. 3 slaves.
Meadow, 10 acres; woodland at 130 pigs.
Odin* holds 4 hides of this land from the Abbot, and Corbelin 2
hides of villagers' land. In lordship 1 plough;
7 villagers and 4 smallholders with 3 ploughs.
A church and another chapel.
*Value of the whole manor before 1066 £16; now, the monks' part   34a
£12 10s; but the men's 60s.

*In WALLINGTON Hundred   33a,b
23 Hamo the Sheriff holds 1½ hides from the Abbot of Chertsey
as a Holding. Alfward held them before 1066; he could turn
where he would. In lordship 1 plough, with
6 cottagers and 3 slaves.
Meadow, 11 acres.
Value before 1066, later and now 20s.

24 Hamo also holds ½ hide from the Abbey itself. Wulfward held it
before 1066; he could turn where he would.
1 cottager.
Meadow, 5 acres.
The value is and was 5s.
These 2 hides which Hamo holds answered for 2 hides before 1066,
now for ½.

In BRIXTON Hundred
25 Hamo also holds TOOTING* from the Abbot of Chertsey.
It answered for 6 hides less 1 virgate before 1066; now for nothing.
Land for 3 ploughs. In lordship 1 plough;
3 villagers and 2 smallholders with 1 plough. A church.
Meadow, 4 acres.
Value before 1066, 40s; later 20s; now 70s.

26 Hamo also holds 1 hide in TOOTING* from the Abbot of Chertsey.
Osward held it from King Edward; he could go where he would.
1 villager with ½ plough.
Meadow, 1 acre.
[Value] before 1066, 15s; now 10s.

In *CERCEFELLE HVND* Willelm de Wateuile tenuit *TEPESTEDE* . de
abbe de Certefy . Turgifus 7 Vlf tenuer T.R.E. Terra Turgifi erat
de abbatia . Vlf poterat ire quo uolebat . Tc fe defdb p.v.hid. modo p una
hida . Ibi funt . II . uilli 7 un bord . Qdo Wills abiit: erat ad firmā de . XL . fo

34 a Vluuin ten de ipfa abbatia *BIFLET* . Ifd tenuit . T.R.E. Tc fe
defd p . VIII . hid . Modo p . II . hid 7 dim . Tra . ē . II . car . In dnio . c
una car . 7 VII . uilli 7 II . bord cū . II . car . Ibi æccla 7 III . ferui .
7 un moliñ de . v . fol . Vna pifcaria 7 dimid de . cccxxv . anguill .
7 VI . ac pti . Silua: de . x . porc . de pafnag . T.R.E: c . fol . m: IIII . lib .
Ipfa abbatia ten *CLANEDVN* . T.R.E. fe defd *IN WOCHINGES HD* .
p . x . hid . modo p . IIII . hid . Tra . ē . v . car . Ibi . VI . uilli 7 XII . bord
cū . VII . car . Silua: de . VI . porc . T.R.E. ualb . VI . lib . Modo: IIII . lib .
7 tam uilli qui ten eā reddt VI . lib .
Abb de Certefy emit T.R.E. in Clanedun . II . hid . 7 mifit in ifto
Anfchil tenuit de rege . Eps baiocfis mifit eas in Brunlei . injufte .
ut hoēs de hund teftant .
Ipfa abbatia ten *HENLEI* . Azor tenuit donec obiit 7 ded æcclæ
p anima fua tpr regis . W. ut dnt monachi . 7 inde hnt breuē regis .
T.R.E. fe defd p . VIII . hid . m p . v . hid 7 dim . Tra . ē . v . car . In dnio
eft . I . car . 7 x . uilli 7 VI . bord cū . v . car . Ibi æccla . 7 II . ferui . 7 IIII . ac
pti . Silua: L . porc de pafnag . T.R.E: ualb . VI . lib . Modo: c . fol .

In REIGATE Hundred

27 William of Watteville held CHIPSTEAD from the Abbot of Chertsey.
Thorgils and Ulf held it before 1066. Thorgils' land was the
Abbey's. Ulf could go where he would. Then it answered for 5
hides, now for 1 hide.
2 villagers and 1 smallholder.
When William went away it was at a revenue of 40s.

In GODLEY Hundred   34a

28 Wulfwin holds BYFLEET from the Abbey itself. He also held it
before 1066. Then it answered for 8 hides; now for 2½ hides.
Land for 2 ploughs. In lordship 1 plough;
7 villagers and 2 smallholders with 2 ploughs.
A church; 3 slaves.
A mill at 5s; 1½ fisheries of 325 eels; meadow, 6 acres;
woodland at 10 pigs from pasturage.
Value before 1066, 100s; now £4.

In WOKING Hundred

29 The Abbey holds (East) CLANDON itself. Before 1066 it answered
for 10 hides; now for 4 hides. Land for 5 ploughs.
6 villagers and 12 smallholders with 7 ploughs.
Woodland at 6 pigs.
Value before 1066 £6; now £4; however, the villagers who
hold it pay £6.
Before 1066 the Abbot of Chertsey bought 2 hides in Clandon* and
put them in this manor. Askell held them from the King.
The Bishop of Bayeux wrongfully put them in Bramley, as the
men of the Hundred testify.

30 The Abbey holds HENLEY itself. Azor held it until he died,
and gave it to the Church for his soul's sake in King William's
time, as the monks say. They have the King's writ for it.
Before 1066 it answered for 8 hides; now for 5½ hides.
Land for 5 ploughs. In lordship 1 plough;
10 villagers and 6 smallholders with 5 ploughs.
A church; 2 slaves.
Meadow, 4 acres; woodland, 50 pigs from pasturage.
Value before 1066 £6; now 100s.

TERRA SCI WANDREGISILI. *IN BRIXIESTAN HD.*

.IX. Abbas S Wandregiſili ten *WANDESORDE* . p Ingulfū monacħ.
Suein tenuit de rege . 7 potuit ire quo uoluit . Tc ſe defđ .p una
hida . m̃ .p nichilo . Ibi ſunt . III . uiħi 7 II . borđ . cū una caŕ . Valuit

TERRA SCI LEVTFREDI. *IN AMELEBRIGE HD.* [xx.ſoł 7 uał.

.X. Abbas de Cruce S Leutfredi ten de dono regis . W. in *AISSELE*
VII . hiđ 7 III . virǵ . træ . Toui tenuit de rege . E.
Tra . e̅ . II . caŕ . In dn̄io . e̅ una . 7 IIII . uiħi 7 XI . cot́ . cū . II . caŕ.
Vał . III . liɓ . Poſtq̄ Scs habuit́ nunq̄ gelđ dedit.

TERRA ÆCCLÆ DE LABATAILGE. *IN TENRIGE HVND.*

.XI. ABBAS De Labatailge ten *LIMENESFELD* . Heralđ tenuit
T . R . E . Tc ſe defđ .p . XXV . hiđ . Modo n̄ ſe defđ p̄q̄ aɓɓ receɓ.
Tra . e̅ . XII . caŕ . In dn̄io ſunt . V . caŕ . 7 XXV . uiħi 7 VI . borđ cū
XIIII . caŕ . Ibi un̄ molin̄ de . II . ſoł . 7 una piſcaria . 7 I . æccła.
7 IIII . ac̄ p̄ti . Silua:́ de CL . porc̀ de paſnag . Due foſſæ Lapidū:́
de . II . ſoł . 7 III . nidi accipitr in ſilua . 7 X . ſerui.
T . R . E . uałɓ . XX . liɓ . 7 poſt:́ XV . liɓ . Modo . XXIIII . liɓ.
Huic ꝳ ptin *BRAMESELLE* . T . R . E . ut hões de hunđ dn̄t.

TERRA ÆCCLÆ DE BERCHINGES. *IN AMELEBRIGE HVND.*

.XIJ. Abbatia de BERCHINGES ħ . VII . hiđ ad *WESTONE* . Modo ſe defđ
.p . III . hiđ 7 una v̄ . Tra . e̅ . III . caŕ . Ibi ſunt . IX . uiħi cū . III . caŕ . Vał
Ipſa abbatia ħ . II . hidas træ *IN WALETONE HD* [XL . ſoł . 7 ualuit.
T . R . E . ſe defđ .p . II . hiđ . modo .p una . Ibi ſunt . II . uiħi . cū dim̃ caŕ.
7 VI . ac̄ p̄ti . T . R . E . uałɓ . I . marħ argenti . Modo:́ XX . ſoł.

34 a

9   LAND OF ST. WANDRILLE'S

In BRIXTON Hundred
1 The Abbot of St. Wandrille's holds WANDSWORTH through the monk
Ingulf. Swein held it from the King, and could go where he would.
Then it answered for 1 hide; now for nothing.
  3 villagers and 2 smallholders with 1 plough.
The value was and is 20s.

10   LAND OF ST. LEUFROY'S

In ELMBRIDGE Hundred
1 The Abbot of [Holy] Cross of St. Leufroy holds 7 hides and 3
virgates of land in ESHER by gift of King William. Tovi held
it from King Edward. Land for 2 ploughs. In lordship 1;
  4 villagers and 11 cottagers with 2 ploughs.
Value £3.
Since Sant [Leufroy's] had it it has never paid tax.

11   LAND OF BATTLE CHURCH

In TANDRIDGE Hundred
1 The Abbot of Battle holds LIMPSFIELD. Harold held it before 1066.
Then it answered for 25 hides. Now since the Abbot acquired it, it
is not answerable. Land for 12 ploughs. In lordship 5 ploughs;
  25 villagers and 6 smallholders with 14 ploughs.
  A mill at 2s; a fishery; a church; meadow, 4 acres;
    woodland at 150 pigs from pasturage; 2 stone quarries at 2s;
    3 hawk's nests in the woodland; 10 slaves.
Value before 1066 £20; later £15; now £24.
  Branshill* (?) belonged to this manor before 1066, as the men
of the Hundred state.

12   LAND OF BARKING CHURCH

In ELMBRIDGE Hundred
1 The Abbey of Barking has 7 hides at WESTON. Now it answers
for 3 hides and 1 virgate. Land for 3 ploughs.
  9 villagers with 3 ploughs.
The value is and was 40s.

In WALLINGTON Hundred
2 The Abbey has 2 hides of land itself. Before 1066 it answered
for 2 hides; now for 1.
  2 villagers with ½ plough.
  Meadow, 6 acres.
Value before 1066, 1 silver mark; now 20s.

TERRA SCI PAVLI LVNDONIENS. *IN BRIXISTAN HVND.*

I
.XII. Canonici S PAVLI Lundon ten *BERNE*. T.R.E. ſe defð ꝑ. viii . hið.
Hæ hidæ geldaueꝛ 7 geldaꝃ cū Mortelage M Archiepi . 7 ibi ſuꝃ
cōputatæ . Tra . e̅ . vi . caꝛ . In dn̅io ſunt . ii . caꝛ . 7 ix . uiłłi 7 iiii . borð
cū . iii . caꝛ . 7 xx . ac̅ pti . T.R.E, uałð . vi . lið . Modo: vii . lið.

TERRA ÆCCLÆ DE LANCHEI. *IN BRIXISTAN HVND.*

II
.XII. SCA MARIA M eſt qð *LANCHEI* uocat̅ . comitiſſa Goda tenuit ſoror . R.E.
34 b Tc̅ ſe defð ꝑ . x . hið . m̅ ꝑ . ii . hið 7 dim̅ . Tra . e̅ . xii . caꝛ.
In dn̅io ſunt . ii . caꝛ . 7 xii . uiłłi 7 xxvii . borð cū . iiii . caꝛ.
Ibi æccła . 7 xix . burgenſes| In Londonia qui reddt̅ . xxxvi . ſoł . 7 ibi . iii.
ſerui . 7 xvi . ac̅ pti . Silua: de . iii . porc̅.
T.R.E. 7 poſt: uał . x . lið . Modo: xi . lið.
De iſto M hꝉ eps baiocꝼis unā culturā træ . quæ antе
7 poſt mortē Godæ jacuit in iſta æccła.

TERRA COMITIS EVSTACHIJ. *IN TENRIGE HVND.*

.XV. Comes EVSTACHIVS ten *ACSTEDE* mat' Heraldi Gida tenuit . T.R.E.
Tc̅ ſe defð ꝑ . xx . hið . Modo ꝑ . v . hið . Tra . e̅ . xx . caꝛ.
In dn̅io ſunt . ii . caꝛ . 7 xxxiiii . uiłłi cū . xviii . caꝛ . Ibi . ii.
M. molini de . xii . ſoł 7 vi . denaꝛ . 7 iiii . ac̅ pti . Silua: c . porc̅
de paſnag . 7 In Suduuerca . i . maſura de . ii . denaꝛ . 7 vi.
ſerui . 7 ix . borð . Ibi æccła.
T.R.E: uałð xvi . lið . Qdo recep: x . lið . Modo: xiiii . lið.
Ipſe comes ten *WACHELESTEDE* . Oſuuard tenuit de rege . E.
Tc̅ ſe defð ꝑ . xl . hið . modo ꝑ . vi . hið Tra . e̅ . xxx . caꝛ.
In dn̅io ſunt . iii . caꝛ . 7 xxxix . uiłłi 7 ii . borð cū . xxii.

13   LAND OF ST. PAUL'S, LONDON

In BRIXTON Hundred

1 The Canons of St. Paul's, London hold BARNES. Before 1066 it
  answered for 8 hides. These hides paid and pay tax with the
  Archbishop's manor of Mortlake*, and are there accounted.
  Land for 6 ploughs. In lordship 2 ploughs;
    10* villagers and 4 smallholders with 3 ploughs.
    Meadow, 20 acres.
  Value before 1066 £6; now £7.

14   LAND OF LAMBETH CHURCH

In BRIXTON Hundred

1 St. Mary's is a manor called LAMBETH. Countess Goda*, King Edward's
  sister held it. Then it answered for 10 hides; now for 2½ hides.   34b
  Land for 12 ploughs. In lordship 2 ploughs;
    12 villagers and 27 smallholders with 4 ploughs. A church;
    19 burgesses in London who pay 36s. 3 slaves.
    Meadow, 16 acres; woodland at 3 pigs.
  Value before 1066 and later £10; now £11.
    The Bishop of Bayeux has one field of this manor, which lay in
  (the lands of) this church before and after Goda's death.

15   LAND OF COUNT EUSTACE

In TANDRIDGE Hundred

1 Count Eustace holds OXTED. Gytha, Harold's mother, held it
  before 1066. Then answered for 20 hides; now for 5 hides.
  Land for 20 ploughs. In lordship 2 ploughs;
    34 villagers with 18 ploughs.
    2 mills at 12s 6d; meadow, 4 acres; woodland, 100 pigs from
      pasturage; in Southwark, 1 dwelling at 2d; 6 slaves;
    9 smallholders; a church.
  Value before 1066 £16; when acquired £10; now £14.

2 The Count holds WALKINGSTEAD* himself. Osward held it from
  King Edward. Then it answered for 40 hides; now for 6 hides.
  Land for 30 ploughs. In lordship 3 ploughs;
    39 villagers and 2 smallholders with 22 ploughs. 10 slaves.

car̄ . Ibi . x . ſerui . 7 uñ moliñ de . vi . ſoł . 7 iii . ac̄ p̄ti.

Silua: de . c . porc̄ . Huic ⏟ p̄tiñ . xv . maſuræ in

Suduuerca . 7 in Londoñ de . vi . ſoł . 7 ii . milleñ alleciū.

T.R.E. uałb xx . lib . 7 poſt: xvi . lib . Modo: xx . lib.

Tam̄ redd . xxviii . lib ad penſā. In Cherchefelle Hd.
.XVI.

Comitiſſa bononienſis ten̄ de rege Notfelle . Vluui

tenuit de rege . E . Tc̄ ſe defd ꝑ . xiii . hid 7 dim̄ . Modo

ꝑ . iii . hid . Tra . ē . xii . car̄ . In dñio ſunt . iii . car̄ . 7 xxv.

uiłłi 7 x . bord cū . xiii . car̄ . Ibi æccła 7 x . ſerui . 7 uñ

moliñ de . ii . ſoł . 7 x . ac̄ p̄ti . De herbagio: xii . porc̄.

T.R.E. uałb . xiii . lib . 7 poſt: x . lib . Modo: xv . lib de xx . in ora.
.XVII.

Terra Comitis Moriton̄. In Brixistan hvnd.

Comes Moriton̄ ten̄ Lanchei . Canonici de Walthā

tenuer̄ de Heraldo . Tc̄ ſe defd ꝑ . vi . hid 7 dim̄ . modo

ꝑ nichilo . Tra . ē . vi . car̄ . In dñio . ē . i . car̄ . 7 v . uiłłi 7 xii.

bord cū . iii . car̄ . Ibi uñ ſeruus . 7 vi . ac̄ p̄ti.

T.R.E. uałb . c . ſoł . 7 poſt 7 m̄: iiii . lib.

Iſd̄e com̄ hr̄ in Bermundeſy de tra regis . i . hid . ubi ſedet

dom ej . Ibi . ē uñ bord . Vał . viii . ſoł . In Waleton hvnd.

Iſd com̄ hr̄ . ii . hid træ 7 unā v de rege . Ailmar tenuit de

rege . E . Modo ñ ſe defd . Ibi ſunt . iiii . uiłłi . 7 ix . cot cū . iii . car̄.

7 ix . ac̄ p̄ti . T.R.E. 7 m̄ . uał . xl . ſoł . Cū recep: xx . ſoł . ꝑ . ii . hid 7 i . v ſe defdbat.

Ipſe com̄ ten̄ Estrehā . T.R.E. ſe defd ꝑ . v . hid . m̄ ꝑ nichilo.

Herald tenuit . i . hid 7 dim̄ . Canonici de Walthā: i . hid 7 dim̄.

Tres ſoch̄i tenuer̄ . ii . hid 7 quo uoluer̄ cū eis ire potuer̄ . Tra . ē . ii . car̄.

Ibi ſunt . iii . uiłłi 7 iii . bord cū . ii . car̄ 7 dim̄.

T.R.E. uałb . xxx . ſoł . 7 poſt: xv . ſoł . Modo: xliii . ſoł.

A mill at 6s; meadow, 3 acres; woodland for 100 pigs.
To this manor belong 15 dwellings in Southwark and in London, at 6s,
and 2000 herrings.
Value before 1066 £20; later £16; now £20; however, it pays
£28 by weight.

16 [LAND OF THE COUNTESS OF BOULOGNE]

In REIGATE Hundred
1 The Countess of Boulogne* holds NUTFIELD from the King.
Wulfwy held it from King Edward. Then it answered for 13½ hides;
now for 3 hides. Land for 12 ploughs. In lordship 3 ploughs;
25 villagers and 10 smallholders with 13 ploughs.
A church; 10 slaves.
A mill at 2s; meadow, 10 acres; from grazing, 12 pigs.
Value before 1066 £13; later £10; now £15, at 20 [pence] to the ora.

17 LAND OF THE COUNT OF MORTAIN

In BRIXTON Hundred
1 The Count of Mortain holds LAMBETH*. The Canons of Waltham held
it from Harold. Then it answered for 6½ hides; now for nothing.
Land for 6 ploughs. In lordship 1 plough;
5 villagers and 12 smallholders with 3 ploughs. 1 slave.
Meadow, 6 acres.
Value before 1066, 100s; later and now £4.

2 The Count also has 1 hide of the King's land in BERMONDSEY*
where his house stands.
1 smallholder.
Value 8s.

In WALLINGTON Hundred
3 The Count also has 2 hides and 1 virgate of land from the King.
Aelmer held it from King Edward. Now it is not answerable.
4 villagers and 9 cottagers with 3 ploughs.
Meadow, 9 acres.
Value before 1066 and now 40s; when acquired 20s.
It answered for 2 hides and 1 virgate.

4 The Count also holds HAM*. Before 1066 it answered for 5 hides;
now for nothing. Harold held 1½ hides; the Canons of
Waltham, 1½ hides. 3 Freemen held 2 hides, and could go
where they would with them. Land for 2 ploughs .
3 villagers and 3 smallholders with 2½ ploughs.
Value before 1066, 30s; later 15s; now 43s.

TERRA COMITIS ROGERIJ. *IN WODETONE HVND.*

.XVI. Comes ROGERIVS hᷓ unā hiđ de rege.quæ jacet in Contone
ⲙ᷎ ej in Sudſexe.T.R.E.qui contone tenuit.iſtā hiđ de rege
tenuit.Tᷓ ſe ᵱ una hida defđ.ᷫ ᵱ nichilo.Ibi.ē in dᷜio.ı.carͧ.
T.R.E.uaᷝ.xx.ſoͷ.7 poſt 7 ᷫ.ͧxv.ſoliđ.

34 c   Turalđ͏᷎ tenͧ de comite Rogeᷓ.*BORHAM*.Oſmunđͧ tenuit
de rege.E.Tᷓ ſe defđ ᵱ.ıııı.hiđ.modo ᵱ.ııı.hiđ.Tra.ē
v.carͧ.In dᷜio.ē una carͧ.7 vıı.uiͷ.7 ıı.borđ.cū.ııı.carͧ.
7 dim.7 uᷜ molī de.xv.ſoliđ.7 xxv.ac̄ p̄ti.Siluaͧde
qᷓͧ ᷑ xxͧ.porc̄ paſnagͧ.Ibi.ıııı.ſerui.
De his hiđ hᷓ Godric̄.ı.hiđ quæ uocat᷎ͧWucha.in qua
fuit haula T.R.E.p̄tin ad iſtū ⲙ᷎.7 ibi.ē in dᷜio.ı.carͧ.
7 ıııı.uiͷ 7 ııı.borđ cū.ı.carͧ.7 uno ſeruo.Silua.de.ııı.porͧc̄.
Toᷓ ⲙ᷎ T.R.E.7 poſt.ͧuaᷝ.vııı.liᷝ.Modo.ͧdᷜs vıı.liᷝ.hᷛ ej.ͧ
Turalđ͏᷎ tenͧ de comͧ *WERPESDVNE*.   ℱ xx.ſoͷ.
Oſmunđ tenuit de rege.E.Tᷓ ſe defđ ᵱ.vııı.hiđ.Modo
ᵱ vı.hiđ 7 dim.Tra.ē.vıı.carͧ.In dᷜio.ē una carͧ.7 xııı.
uiͷ 7 ııı.borđ.cū.vı.carͧ.Ibi æccͷa.7 uᷜ͏᷎ ſeru͏᷎.7 vııı.ac̄ p̄ti.
Silua.ͧʟx.porc̄ de paſnag.
De hac traͧ tenͧ͏᷎ duo milites.ıı.hiđ 7 unā vͧ.7 ibi hᷜt in dᷜio
.ıı.carͧ.7 ııı.uiͷos 7 ıı.borđ.7 uᷜ molī de.xxx.denarͧ.
Totͧ.T.R.E.ᶴuaᷝ.x.liᷝ.Modo ſimiliᷓ x.liᷝ inᷓ totū.
Turolđ tenͧ de comͧ *LOSELE*.Oſmunđ͏᷎ *IN GODELMINGE HĐ.*
tenuit de rege.E.Tᷓ ſe defđ ᵱ.ııı.hiđ.Modo ᵱ.ıı.hiđ.
Tra.ē.ıı.carͧ.In dᷜio.ē una carͧ.7 vıı.uiͷ 7.ı.ͧcoᷓ cū.ııı.
carͧ.Ibi.ıı.ſerui.7 v.ac̄ p̄ti.T.R.E.uaᷝ.xʟ.ſoͷ.7 poſt.ͧxx.ſoͷ.
               ℱ Modo.ͧʟx.ſoͷ.

In WOTTON Hundred
1 Earl Roger has 1 hide from the King, which lies in (the lands of) his
   manor of COMPTON in Sussex*. Before 1066 the holder of Compton
   held this hide from the King. Then it answered for 1 hide; now
   for nothing. In lordship 1 plough.
   Value before 1066, 20s; later and now 15s.

[In WOKING Hundred]   34c
2 Thorold holds BURPHAM from Earl Roger. Osmund held it from
   King Edward. Then it answered for 4 hides, now for 3 hides.
   Land for 5 ploughs. In lordship 1 plough;
      7 villagers and 2 smallholders with 3½ ploughs.
      1 mill at 15s; meadow, 25 acres; woodland at 80 pigs
         pasturage. 4 slaves.
   Of these hides Godric has 1 hide called WYKE, in which was the hall,
   which belonged to this manor before 1066. In lordship 1 plough;
      4 villagers and 3 smallholders with 1 plough and 1 slave.
      Woodland at 3 pigs.
   Value of the whole manor before 1066 and later £8;
   now, the lord £7, his man 20s.

3 Thorold holds WORPLESDON from the Earl. Osmund held it from
   King Edward. Then it answered for 8 hides, now for 6½ hides.
   Land for 7 ploughs. In lordship 1 plough;
      13 villagers and 3 smallholders with 6 ploughs.
      A church; 1 slave.
      Meadow, 8 acres; woodland, 60 pigs from pasturage.
   2 men-at-arms hold 2 hides and 1 virgate of this land.
   In lordship they have 2 ploughs, and
      3 villagers and 2 smallholders;
      1 mill at 30d.
   Total value before 1066 and later £10; now the same, £10 in all.

In GODALMING Hundred
4 Thorold holds LOSELEY from the Earl. Osmund held it from
   King Edward. Then it answered for 3 hides, now for 2 hides.
   Land for 2 ploughs. In lordship 1 plough;
      7 villagers and 1 cottager with 3 ploughs. 2 slaves.
      Meadow, 5 acres.
   Value before 1066, 40s; later 20s; now 60s.

.XIX. RICARDVS DE TONEBRIGE teñ in dñio *CIVENTONE.*

Alnod tenuit de rege . E . Tc̄ ſe defð ᵱ . xx . hið . m̃

ᵱ . vi . hið . Tra . ē . xii . car̄ . In dñio ſunt . ii . car̄ 7 dimið.

7 xxiii . uilli 7 uñ borð cũ . ix . car̄ . Ibi . ix . ſerui . 7 uñ moliñ

de . xxxii . denar̄ . De herbag: xii . porc̄ . Silua: de . L . porc̄

de paſnag . 7 xvi . ãc p̃ti.

De his hið teñ Rogeri dimið hidã . 7 ibi hr̄ in dñio . i . car̄ . cũ . v.

borð . In Sudwerche . iii . hag de xv . deñ . 7 in Lundoñ . ii . maˢ

ſuras de . x . deñ . T.R.E. ualb̄ xi . lib̄ . 7 poſt: vi . lib̄ . Modo: x . lib̄.

Ipſe Ricard teñ *BLACHINGELEI* . Ælfech 7 Aluuiñ 7 Elnod

tenuer̄ de rege . E . Tc̄ ſe defð ᵱ . x . hið . Modo ᵱ . iii . hið.

Tra . ē . xvi . car̄ . Tria ⊕ fuer̄ . modo . ē in unũ . In dñio ſunt

iii . car̄ . 7 xx . uilli 7 iiii . borð cũ . ix . car̄ . Ibi . vii . ſerui.

7 xiiii , ãc p̃ti . De ſilua: xL . porc̄ . 7 de herbag . xviii . porc̄.

In Lundonia . vii . manſuræ de . v . ſol 7 iiii . deñ.
⁷ Sudwerche

De his . x . hið teñ Odm̃ . ii . hið . 7 Lemei . ii . 7 Petr̄ . i . hið 7 dim̄.

In dñio . i . car̄ . 7 iii . uilli 7 ii . borð cũ . i . car̄ . 7 iii . ãc p̃ti.

Toẽ ⊕ T.R.E. ualb̄ . xiii . lib̄ . 7 poſt: viii . lib̄ . Modo qð teñ

Ricard: xii . lib̄ . Qð hoēs ej: Lxxiii . ſol 7 iiii . deñ.

Robt̄ de Wateuile teñ de Ricardo *CELESHAM.*

Vluuard tenuit de rege . E . Tc̄ ſe defð ᵱ . x . hið . modo

ᵱ . ii . hið . Tra . ē . iiii . car̄ . In dñio ſunt . ii . car̄ . 7 vi . uilli

7 xi . borð . cũ . iii . car̄ . Ibi . iiii . ſerui . De c̄ſuetudine: i . porc̄.

T.R.E. ualb̄ . vi . lib̄ . 7 poſt: iii . lib̄ . Modo: viii . lib̄.

34 b Vxor Salie teñ de Ricardo *TENRIGE* . Torbern

tenuit de rege . E . Tc̄ ſe defð ᵱ . x . hið . m̃ ᵱ . ii . hið.

Tra . ē . x . car̄ . In dñio ſunt . iii . car̄ . 7 xx . uilli 7 x . borð.

19   LAND OF RICHARD SON OF COUNT GILBERT

In TANDRIDGE Hundred

1 Richard of Tonbridge holds CHIVINGTON in lordship. Alnoth held it
from King Edward. Then it answered for 20 hides, now for 6 hides.
Land for 12 ploughs. In lordship 2½ ploughs;
   23 villagers and 1 smallholder with 9 ploughs. 9 slaves.
A mill at 32d; from grazing, 12 pigs; woodland at 50 pigs
   from pasturage; meadow, 16 acres.
Of these hides, Roger holds ½ hide. He has in lordship 1 plough with
5 smallholders. In Southwark, 3 sites at 15d; in London
   2 dwellings at 10d.
Value before 1066 £11; later £6; now £10.

2 Richard holds BLECHINGLEY himself. Alfheah, Alwin and Alnoth held
it from King Edward. Then it answered for 10 hides, now for 3 hides.
Land for 16 ploughs. There were three manors; now it is in one.
In lordship 3 ploughs;
   20 villagers and 4 smallholders with 9 ploughs. 7 slaves.
Meadow, 14 acres; from the woodland, 40 pigs; from grazing,
   18 pigs. In London and Southwark, 7 dwellings at 5s 4d.
Of these 10 hides Odin* holds 2½ hides, Leofmer* 2 hides,
and Peter 1½ hides. In lordship 1 plough;
   3 villagers and 2 smallholders with 1 plough.
Meadow, 3 acres.
Value of the whole manor before 1066 £13; later £8; now
what Richard holds £12; what his men hold 73s 4d.

3 Robert of Watteville holds CHELSHAM from Richard. Wulfward held
it from King Edward. Then it answered for 10 hides, now for 2
hides. Land for 4 ploughs. In lordship 2 ploughs;
   6 villagers and 11 smallholders with 3 ploughs. 4 slaves.
   From customary dues, 1 pig.
Value before 1066 £6; later £3; now £8.

4 Salie's wife holds TANDRIDGE from Richard. Thorbern held it   34d
from King Edward. Then it answered for 10 hides, now for 2 hides.
Land for 10 ploughs. In lordship 3 ploughs;
   20 villagers and 10 smallholders with 11 ploughs.

cū . xı . car̄ . Ibi . ı . molin dc . ʟ . den . 7 v . āc p̄ti . Silua: xʟ . porc̄

de pafnag . De herbag . xı . porc̄.

T.R.E . ualb . vı . lib . 7 poft: xʟ . fol . Modo: xı . lib.

Ipfa ead uxor Salie tēn de Ricardo *TELLINGEDONE* . Alnod

tenuit dc rege . E . Tc̄ fe defd ꝑ . x . hid . modo ꝑ una hid 7 dim.

Tra . ē . ıııı . car̄ . In dn̄io funt . ıı . car̄ . 7 v . uiłłi 7 vııı . ſerui . cū . ıı.

car̄ 7 dim. Ibi æccła . Silua . dc . xxx . porc̄ pafnag.

T.R.E . ualb . vıı . lib . 7 poft . ııı . lib . M: vı . lib . 7 tam̄ redd . vıı . lib.

Robt de Wateuile tēn de Ricardo un̄ maneriū

Qd Azor tenuit de rege . E . Tc̄ fe defd ꝑ . xıııı . hid . m̄ ꝑ . ıı . hid.

Tra . ē . ıııı . car̄ . In dn̄io funt . ıı . car̄ . 7 xı . uiłłi 7 vıı . bord cū . ııı.

car̄ . Silua: v . porc̄ de pafnag . Ibi æccła.

T.R.E . 7 m̄: ual . vııı . lib . Cū recep̄: c . fol.

Isdē Robt tēn de Ricardo *CHELESHA* . Tochi tenuit de rege . E.

Tc̄ fe defd ꝑ . x . hid . m̄ ꝑ . ıı . hid . Tra . ē . ıııı . car̄ . In dn̄io funt . ıı.

7 xı . uiłłi 7 vıı . bord . cū . ıııı . car̄ . Ibi æccła 7 ııı . ſerui.

T.R.E . 7 m̄ ual . vıı . lib . Cū recep̄: ıııı . lib.

Isdē Robt tēn de Ricardo *FERLEGA* . Toui tenuit de rege . E.

Tc̄ fe defd ꝑ . vı . hid . m̄ ꝑ dimid hida . Tra . ē . ıı . car̄ 7 dim.

In dn̄io . ē una . 7 ıııı . uiłłi . 7 ı . bord . cū una car̄ . Ibi . ı . ſeru . 7 ı . bos.

T.R.E . 7 m̄ ual ʟx . fol . Cū recep̄: xx . fol.

Johs tēn de Ricardo *WALLINGEHA* . Vlftan tenuit de

rege . E . Tc̄ fe defd ꝑ . vııı . hid . Modo ꝑ una . Tra . ē

In dn̄io . ē una car̄ 7 dim . 7 vı . uiłłi 7 ııı . bord cū . ııı . car̄ . Ibi.

ııı . ſerui .   T.R.E . 7 m̄ . ual . ıııı . lib . Cū recep̄: xx . fol.

Sc̄a Maria de bech tēn   *IN BRIXIESTAN HVND.*

de dono Ricardi *TOTINGES* . Eftarcher tenuit de rege . E . Tc̄ fe

defd ꝑ . xı . hid . 7 m̄ | fimilit . Tra . ē . ıııı . car̄ . In dn̄io funt . ıı . car̄ . 7 v.

uiłłi 7 ıııı . bord . cū . ııı . car̄ . Ibi . x . āc p̄ti.

T.R.E . 7 m̄ . ual . c . fol . Cū recep̄: xx . fol.

1 mill at 50d; meadow, 5 acres; woodland, 40 pigs from
pasturage; from grazing, 11 pigs.
Value before 1066 £6; later 40s; now £11.

5 Salie's wife also holds TILLINGDON herself from Richard. Alnoth
held it from King Edward. Then it answered for 10 hides,
now for 1½ hides. Land for 4 ploughs. In lordship 2 ploughs;
5 villagers and 8 slaves with 2½ ploughs. A church.
Woodland at 30 pigs pasturage.
Value before 1066 £7; later £3; now £6; however, it pays £7.

6 Robert of Watteville holds one manor* from Richard, which Azor held
from King Edward. Then it answered for 14 hides, now for 2 hides.
Land for 4 ploughs. In lordship 2 ploughs;
11 villagers and 7 smallholders with 3 ploughs.
Woodland, 5 pigs from pasturage. A church.
Value before 1066 and now £8; when acquired 100s.

7 Robert also holds CHELSHAM from Richard. Toki held it from King
Edward. Then it answered for 10 hides, now for 2 hides. Land
for 4 ploughs. In lordship 2;
11 villagers and 7 smallholders with 4 ploughs.
A church; 3 slaves.
Value before 1066 and now £7; when acquired £4.

8 Robert also holds FARLEIGH from Richard. Tovi held it from King
Edward. Then it answered for 6 hides, now for ½ hide.
Land for 2½ ploughs. In lordship 1;
4 villagers and 1 smallholder with 1 plough; 1 slave.
1 ox.
Value before 1066 and now 60s; when acquired 20s.

9 John holds WOLDINGHAM from Richard. Wulfstan held it from King
Edward. Then it answered for 8 hides, now for 1. Land for ....
In lordship 1½ ploughs;
6 villagers and 3 smallholders with 3 ploughs. 3 slaves.
Value before 1066 and now £4; when acquired 20s.

In BRIXTON Hundred
10 St. Mary's of Bec* holds TOOTING (Bec) by gift of Richard.
Starker held it from King Edward. Then it answered for 11 hides,
now for 1 hide*. Land for 4 ploughs. In lordship 2 ploughs;
5 villagers and 4 smallholders with 3 ploughs.
Meadow, 10 acres.
Value before 1066 and now 100s; when acquired 20s.

Ipſa eađ æccła teñ de Ricardo *ESTREHĀ*. Erding tenuit de
rege. E. Tc̄ ſe defđ p̄. v. hiđ. 7 m̄| ſimiliꝛ. ^p·I·hiđ⁷⁷·I·v·ꞇer⁹·⁊ Tra. ē. III. car̄. In dñio. ē
una car̄. 7 IIII. uiłłi 7 v. borđ. cū. II. car̄. Ibi una capella redđ
VIII. ſoł. Ibi. IIII. ac̄ p̄ti. Silua. de x. porc̄. p̄ herbagio: uñ porc̄
de. x. porc̄. T. R. E. uałꝗ. L. ſoł. 7 poſt. 7 modo: LX. ſoliđ.

Wiłłs nepos Walchelini ep̄i teñ *IN CHERCHEFELLE HVND*.
de Ricardo *TEPESTEDE*. Vlnod tenuit de rege. E. Tc̄ ſe defđ p̄ xv.
hiđ. modo p̄. II. hiđ. Tra. ē. VII. car̄. In dñio ſunt. II. 7 VIII. uiłłi
7 v. borđ cū. v. car̄. Ibi. v. ſerui. 7 uñ moliñ de. xx. ſoł. Silua: v.
porc̄. aliud nem̄ ſibi retinuit Ricard.

T. R. E. uałꝗ. VII. liꝗ. 7 poſt: c. ſoł. Modo: VI. liꝗ.

Siuuard teñ de Ricardo *ORDE*. Oſuuol tenuit de rege. E. p̄ dim̄
hida ſe defđ tc̄ 7 m̄. Ibi. ē un̄ uiłłs cū dim̄ car̄.

T. R. E. uałꝗ. xxx. ſoł. 7 poſt: II. ſoł. Modo: xx. ſoliđ.

Joħs teñ de Ricardo *BOCHELANT*. Alnod tenuit de rege. E. Tc̄ ſe
defđ p̄. v. hiđ. m̄ p̄. II. hiđ. Tra. ē   In dñio. ē una car̄ 7 dim̄.
7 xVII. uiłłi 7 VIII. borđ cū. x. car̄. Ibi æccła 7 x. ſerui. 7 uñ moliñ
de. VI. ſoł. T. R. E. 7 poſt. uał. c. ſoł. Modo: VIII. liꝗ. *IN WALETON HD*.

Roꝗt de Wateuile ^Ricardo ⁊ de teñ *BEDDINTONE*. Azor tenuit de rege. E.
Tc̄ ſe defđ p̄ xxv. hiđ. m̄ p̄. III. hiđ. Tra. ē. VI. car̄. In dñio. ē una car̄.

35 a 7 xVI. uiłłi 7 xIIII. coꞇ cū. v. car̄. Ibi æccła 7 v. ſerui. 7 II. moliñ
de. xL. ſoł. 7 xxIIII. ac̄ p̄ti. Silua. v. porc̄. In Lundonia. xv.
maſuræ. quæ p̄tiñ huic c̄. redđt. xII. ſoł 7 III. den.

T. R. E. 7 modo. uał. x. liꝗ. Qdo recep̄: VI. liꝗ.

11 This church also holds STREATHAM from Richard. Harding held
   it from King Edward. Then it answered for 5 hides, now for 1
   hide and 1 virgate of land*. Land for 3 ploughs. In lordship 1 plough;
   4 villagers and 5 smallholders with 2 ploughs.
       A chapel which pays 8s.
   Meadow, 4 acres; woodland at 10 pigs; for grazing 1 pig
       in 10 pigs.
   Value before 1066,50s; later and now 60s.

In REIGATE Hundred
12 William, nephew of Bishop Walkelin, holds CHIPSTEAD from Richard.
   Wulfnoth held it from King Edward. Then it answered for 15 hides,
   now for 2 hides. Land for 7 ploughs. In lordship 2;
       8 villagers and 5 smallholders with 5 ploughs. 5 slaves.
   A mill at 20s; woodland, 5 pigs. Richard kept another wood
       for himself.
   Value before 1066 £7; later 100s; now £6.

13 Siward holds WORTH* from Richard. Oswald held it from King
   Edward. It answered for ½ hide, then and now.
       1 villager with ½ plough.
   Value before 1066, 30s; later 2s; now 20s.

14 John holds BUCKLAND from Richard. Alnoth held it from King Edward.
   Then it answered for 5 hides, now for 2 hides. Land for ....
   In lordship 1½ ploughs;
       17 villagers and 8 smallholders with 10 ploughs.
       A church; 10 slaves.
       A mill at 6s.
   Value before 1066 and later 100s; now £8.

In WALLINGTON Hundred
15 Robert of Watteville holds BEDDINGTON from Richard. Azor held it
   from King Edward. Then it answered for 25 hides, now for 3 hides.
   Land for 6 ploughs. In lordship 1 plough;
       16 villagers and 14 cottagers with 5 ploughs. A church; 5 slaves.   35a
   2 mills at 40s; meadow, 24 acres; woodland, 5 pigs. In
       London 15 dwellings which belong to this manor pay 12s 3d.
   Value before 1066 and now £10; when acquired £6.

Ipſe Ricard ten in dñio *ODEMERESTOR* . Azor tenuit de

rege . E . Tĉ 7 m̃ ſe defđ ҏ . xv . hiđ . ſed nunq̃ geldũ dedit.

Tra . ē . iii . car . In dñio ſunt . ii . car . 7 un uiłts 7 xii . cot cũ . iii .

car . Ibi xviii . ſerui . 7 æccła 7 uñ moliñ de . xx . ſoł . 7 iiii . aĉ

p̃ti . Silua : de . x . porc . T . R . E . uałƀ . x . liƀ . 7 poſt :̓ c . ſoł . M̊ . viii . liƀ.

Joħs ten de Ricardo *WALTONE* . IN *COPEDEDORNE HVND*.

Aluuin 7 Leſelm 7 Coleman tenuer̃ de rege . E . ҏ . iii . man.

7 potuer̃ ire quo uoluer̃ . Tĉ ſe defđ ҏ xv . hiđ . Modo ҏ . ii.

hiđ 7 dimiđ v̊ . Tra . ē . v . car . In dñio ſunt . ii . car 7 dimiđ.

7 x . uiłti 7 i . borđ cũ . ii . car . 7 vii . ſerui.   Suduuerche.

De his hiđ ten Roger . ii . hiđ . 7 ibi ħ . i . car . 7 i . maſura in

Toť T . R . E . uałƀ . vi . liƀ . 7 poſt :̓ vi . liƀ . Modo :̓ vi . liƀ.

Ipſe Ricard ten de rege unã hidã IN *AMELEBRIGE HĎ*.

quã tenuit Almær de rege . E . 7 potuit cũ ea ire q̃ uoluit.

Nunq̃ gelđ deđ . p q̃ Ricard habuit . Vał . vi . ſoł 7 ix . denar.

Oſuuold ten de Ricardo *MICHELHA* IN *COPEDEDORNE HĎ*.

Iſđe tenuit de rege . E . Tĉ ſe defđ ҏ . v . hiđ . m̃ ҏ . ii . hiđ.

Tra . ē . v . car . In dñio . ē . i . car . 7 viii . uiłti 7 vi . borđ cũ . iiii.

car . Ibi . ii . ſerui . 7 una aĉ p̃ti . 7 uñ porc de paſnag ſiluæ

T . R . E . uałƀ . c . ſoł . Modo :̓ vi . liƀ . IN *CHINGESTVN HĎ*.

Picot ten de Ricardo *TALEORDE* . Aluuin tenuit de rege . E . 7 quo

uoluit ire potuit . Tĉ ſe defđ ҏ . v . hiđ.   Tra . ē . iii . car.

In dñio ſunt . ii . car . 7 vii . uiłti 7 viii . borđ . cũ . iii . car . Ibi . vii.

ſerui . 7 uñ moliñ ſine cenſu . 7 v . aĉ 7 dim p̃ti . 7 dimiđ v̊.

T . R . E . 7 modo :̓ uał . lx . ſoł . Cũ recep :̓ xx . ſoł.

Picot ten de Ricardo . *DITVNE* . Almar tenuit de rege . E.

Tĉ ſe defđ ҏ . v . hiđ . Modo ħ tra 7 ſupior ſe defđ ҏ . iiii . hiđ.

16 Richard holds WOODMANSTERNE himself in lordship. Azor held it
from King Edward. Then and now it answered for 15 hides, but it
never paid tax. Land for 3 ploughs. In lordship 2 ploughs;
1 villager and 12 cottagers with 3 ploughs. 18 slaves; a church.
A mill at 20s; meadow, 4 acres; woodland at 10 pigs.
Value before 1066 £10; later 100s; now £8.

In COPTHORNE Hundred
17 John holds WALTON (-on-the-Hill) from Richard. Alwin, Leofhelm
and Colman held it from King Edward as three manors; they could go
where they would. Then it answered for 15 hides, now for 2 hides
and ½ virgate. Land for 5 ploughs. In lordship 2½ ploughs;
10 villagers and 1 smallholder with 2 ploughs; 7 slaves.
Of these hides Roger holds 2 hides, and has 1 plough.
1 dwelling in Southwark.
Total value before 1066 £6; later £6; now £6.

In ELMBRIDGE Hundred
18 Richard holds 1 hide himself from the King which Aelmer held from
King Edward; he could go where he would with it. It has never
paid tax since Richard had it.
Value 6s 9d.

In COPTHORNE Hundred
19 Oswald holds MICKLEHAM from Richard. He also held it from King
Edward. Then it answered for 5 hides, now for 2 hides.
Land for 5 ploughs. In lordship 1 plough;
8 villagers and 6 smallholders with 4 ploughs. 2 slaves.
Meadow, 1 acre; 1 pig from woodland pasturage.
Value before 1066, 100s; now £6.

In KINGSTON Hundred
20 Picot holds TOLWORTH from Richard. Alwin held it from King
Edward; he could go where he would. Then it answered for 5 hides.*
Land for 3 ploughs. In lordship 2 ploughs;
7 villagers and 8 smallholders with 3 ploughs. 7 slaves.
A mill without dues; meadow, 5½ acres and ½ rod.*
Value before 1066 and now 60s; when acquired 20s.

21 Picot holds (Long) DITTON from Richard. Aelmer held it from King
Edward. Then it answered for 5 hides; now this land, and that

Tra . ē . iiii . car . In dñio . ē . i . car . 7 ii . uilli 7 ix . bord . cū . ii.

car 7 dim . Ibi æccła 7 molin de . ix . soł . Silua de . xv . porc.

Ibi . i . seru . 7 in Sudwerche . i . masura . redd q̄ngent allec.

T.R.E. uałb . lx . soł . 7 post: xxx . soł . Modo: l . soł . Tam est

ad firmā: ꝓ . iiii . lib.

Picot ten de Ricardo unā trā quæ uocat LIMEVRDE . Eduin⁹

tenuit 7 alt hō . T.R.E. 7 potuer ire quo uoluer . Tc se defd

ꝓ dim hida . m̄ ꝓ nichil . Ibi sunt . vi . boues arantes cū . ii . bord.

Robt de Wateuile ten de Ricardo MELDONE . ſ Vał . v . soł sēp.

Erding tenuit de rege . E . Tc se defd ꝓ . viii . hid . Modo ꝓ . iiii.

Tra . ē . v . car . In dñio . ē una car . 7 xiiii . uilli 7 ii . bord cū . iiii.

car . Ibi capella 7 iii . serui . 7 un molin de . xii . soł . 7 iiii . ac

p̄ti . De herbagio: un porc de . vii . porc.

De his hid ten un miles . i . hid 7 unā v . 7 ibi hr . i . car . 7 i . uillm

7 un bord 7 . i . acm p̄ti . Tot T.R.E. uałb . vii . lib . 7 post: c . soł.

Modo: vi . lib 7 xii . solid.

Isde Robt ten de Ricardo CISENDONE . Erding tenuit

de rege . E . Tc se defd ꝓ . v . hid . Modo ꝓ dim hida . Tra . ē.

ii . car . Ibi sunt . iii . uilli 7 un bord cū . i . car . 7 dim molin

35 b   de . ii . soł . Silua de . xxx . porc.

T.R.E. uałb . iiii . lib . 7 post: xl . soł . Modo: lxx . soł.

Vna hida in MELDONE reman in Calengio . quā ten

Robt de Wateuile . 7 dñt hōes de hund qd Eduuard⁹ ^Sarisberie

7 Robt de Oilgi diratiocinauer eā Ricardo de Tonebrige.

7 remansit quieta in manu regis . IN AMELEBRIGE HD.

Ipse Ricard ten WALETONE . Erding tenuit de rege . E.

Tc se defd ꝓ . vi . hid . modo ꝓ . iii . hid . Tra . ē . viii . car.

In dñio sunt . ii . car . 7 viii . uilli 7 iii . cot cū . iii . car.

above answers for 4 hides. Land for 4 ploughs. In lordship 1 plough;
  2 villagers and 9 smallholders with 2½ ploughs. A church.
  A mill at 9s; woodland for 15 pigs; 1 slave; in Southwark
    1 dwelling pays 500 herrings.
Value before 1066, 60s; later 30s; now 50s; however, it is
at a revenue of £4.

22 Picot holds from Richard a land* called 'IMMERWORTH'.* Edwin and
  another man held it before 1066; they could go where they would.
  Then it answered for ½ hide, now for nothing. 6 oxen ploughing, with
    2 smallholders.
  Value always 5s.

23 Robert of Watteville holds MALDEN from Richard. Harding held
  it from King Edward. Then it answered for 8 hides, now for 4.
  Land for 5 ploughs. In lordship 1 plough;
    14 villagers and 2 smallholders with 4 ploughs.
      A chapel; 3 slaves.
      A mill at 12s; meadow, 4 acres; from grazing, 1 pig in 7 pigs.
  Of these hides a man-at-arms holds 1 hide and 1 virgate;
  he has 1 plough, and
    1 villager and 1 smallholder.
    Meadow, 1 acre.
  Total value before 1066 £7; later 100s; now £6 12s.

24 Robert also holds CHESSINGTON from Richard. Harding held it
  from King Edward. Then it answered for 5 hides, now for ½ hide.
  Land for 2 ploughs.
    3 villagers and 1 smallholder with 1 plough.
    ½ mill at 2s; woodland at 30 pigs.
  Value before 1066 £4; later 40s; now 70s.

35b

25 In MALDEN 1 hide, which Robert of Watteville holds, remains in
  dispute. The men of the Hundred state that Edward of Salisbury
  and Robert d'Oilly adjudged it to* Richard of Tonbridge.
  It remains exempt, in the King's hand.

  In ELMBRIDGE Hundred
26 Richard holds WALTON (-on-Thames) himself. Harding held it
  from King Edward. Then it answered for 6 hides, now for 3 hides.
  Land for 8 ploughs. In lordship 2 ploughs;
    8 villagers and 3 cottagers with 3 ploughs. A church.

Ibi æccła . 7 uñ moliñ de . xii . soł 7 vi . deñ . 7 piscaria de

.v . solid . T . R . E . uałb . viii . lib . 7 post . c . soł . Modo. xiiii . lib.

Isdē Ricard hř . vi . hid in ꝏ EBSA . quas abb Wluuold

deliberauit ei in emdatione Waletone . sic hōēs Ricardi

dñt . Sed hōēs de hunđ dūt se nunꝗ uidisse breuē

uel liberatorē regis qui eū inde saisisset . Hanc trā tenuer

nouē teigni . 7 cū ea se poterant uertere quo uolebaɴ .

Ibi sunt . x . uiłłi 7 vi . cot . cū . iiii . cot . Ibi . ii . serui . 7 xlvi .

ac pti . Silua. de . vi . porc .

T . R . E . uałb . iii . lib . 7 post . xl . soł . Modo. iiii . lib.

In Ebsa teñ uñ uiłłs dimiđ hiđ . de qua usꝗ nc deđ hōibȝ

Ricardi . xxx . deñ de gablo . Modo reman ꝗeta in manu

regis . 7 Picot teñ de Ricardo In Ebsa dim hiđ . quā tenuit

Ælmar sine dono regis . eo qđ antecessor ej Ælmar tenuit

teñ nc Picot . Nc uał . v . solid . Præterea teñ Picot de Ri

cardo jn Ebsa dimiđ hidā . quā tenuit Ælmar T . R . E .

7 cū ea potuit ire ꝗlibet . Nc uał . xii . soł .

Joħs teñ de Ricardo MOLESHĀ . Aluric tenuit de rege . E .

Tc se desđ ꝑ . iii . hiđ 7 dimiđ . 7 m̄ ꝑ . v . uirg . Tra . ē . iii .

car . In dñio . ē una car . 7 vii . uiłłi 7 viii . borđ . cū . ii . car .

7 dim . Ibi . xvi . ac pti . Silua de . iiii . porc .

T . R . E . 7 modo. uałb . lx . soł . Cū recep. xl . soł .

In isto ꝏ teñ Joħs de Ricardo . i . hiđ . quæ data fuit

in emdatione Waletone . Vluuard tenuit de rege . E .

Ibi sunt . ii . uiłłi cū . ii . bob . Vał 7 ualuit . v . soł .

Rogeri de Abernon teñ de Ricardo MOLESHAM .

Toco tenuit de rege . E . Tc se desđ ꝑ . vi . hiđ |m̄ ꝑ . vi . uirg .

Tra . ē . iii . car . In dñio . ē una car . 7 iiii . uiłłi 7 iiii . cot

cū . ii . car 7 dimiđ . Ibi . vi . serui . 7 xvi . ac pti . 7 silua.

vi . porc . T . R . E . uałb . iii . lib . 7 post . xl . soł . Modo. lxx . soł .

A mill at 12s 6d; a fishery at 5s.
Value before 1066 £8; later 100s; now £14.

27 Richard also has 6 hides in the manor of APPS which Abbot Wulfwold
(of Chertsey) released to him in compensation for Watton.
So Richard's men say; but the men of the Hundred say that they
have never seen the King's writ or a deliverer who put him in
possession of it. 9 thanes held this land and could
turn where they would with it.
   10 villagers and 6 cottagers with 4 [ploughs] *. 2 slaves.
   Meadow, 46 acres; woodland at 6* pigs.
   Value before 1066 £3; later 40s; now £4.

28 In APPS 1 villager holds ½ hide from which he has hitherto
paid 30d in tribute to Richard's men. Now it remains exempt
in the King's hand, and Picot holds from Richard.
   In Apps, Picot now holds ½ hide which Aelmer held without
the King's gift, because his predecessor Aelmer held it.
   Value now 5s.
   Moreover Picot holds ½ hide in Apps from Richard, which Aelmer
held before 1066; he could go wherever he would with it.
   Value now 12s.

29 John holds (East) MOLESEY from Richard. Aelfric held it from King
Edward. Then it answered for 3½ hides, now for 5 virgates. Land
for 3 ploughs. In lordship 1 plough;
   7 villagers and 8 smallholders with 2½ ploughs.
   Meadow, 16 acres; woodland at 4 pigs.
   Value before 1066 and now 60s; when acquired 40s.

30 In this manor John holds 1 hide from Richard, which was given in
compensation for Walton. Wulfward held it from King Edward.
   2 villagers with 2 oxen.
   The value is and was 5s.

31 Roger d'Abernon holds (East) MOLESEY from Richard. Toki held
it from King Edward. Then it answered for 6½ hides, now
for 6 virgates. Land for 3 ploughs. In lordship 1 plough;
   4 villagers and 4 cottagers with 2½ ploughs. 6 slaves.
   Meadow, 16 acres; woodland, 6 pigs.
   Value before 1066 £3; later 40s; now 70s.

Ipſe Ricard ten STOCHE. Bricſi tenuit de rege.E.

Tc ſe defd p.xv.hid.modo p.11.hid. 7 v.acris.Tra.e vi.car.

In dnio ſunt.11.car. 7 x.uitti 7 ix.cot cu.11.car. Ibi æccta.

7 vii.ſerui. 7 un molin de.vii.ſolid, 7 1111.ac pti.Silua.'
de.xl.porc.T.R.E. 7 m uat.1111.lib.Cu recep.'111.lib.

In eod co ht iſd Ricard, v.hid, Otho tenuit de rege.E.

Modo p dim hida ſe defd.Ibi ſunt.11,uitti cu.vi.bob.

7 un molin de.vi.ſot.Tra.e.11.car.Vat 7 ualuit.xx.ſot.

In DRITEHA ten Ricard.1.hid 7 dim IN FINGEHA HVND.

Ælmar tenuit de rege.E.p uno co.Vxor Salie ten de

35 c Ricardo, 7 ibi ht un uittm 7 11.bord.Valuit, xl, ſot.'m.xxx.ſot.

In ead DRITEHA eſt.1.hida 7 dim qua tenuit Aluric de rege
.E.p uno co. 7 poſtea ded illa tra uxori ſuæ ac filiæ ad æcctam
de Certeſy.ſicuti hoes de hund teſtant.Ricard hanc ca
luniatt Non jacet ulli co.nec p co tenet.ſ; libata fuit ei.

7 modo.111.hidæ geldant p una hida 7 dimid.Tra.e.11.car.
In hac tra.e in dnio.1.car. 7 11.bord. 7 11.ſerui.Vat.xl.ſot.

Rogeri ten de Ricardo ELDEBERIE. IN BLACHEATFELD HD

Azor tenuit de rege.E.Tc ſe defd p.1111.hid.m p.11.hid.

7 dim.Tra.e.vi.car.In dnio.e una. 7 xi.uitti 7 v.bord
cu.vi.car.Ibi æccta. 7 1111.ſerui. 7 molin de.v.ſot.Silua.'
de.xxx.porc.

De his hid ten un miles.1.hid. 7 ibi.in dnio.1.car 7 dim. 7 un
uittm 7 1.ſeruu. 7 una ac pti.

Tot.T.R.E.uatb.x.lib. 7 poſt.'c.ſot.Modo.ix.lib.

32 Richard holds STOKE (d'Abernon) himself. Young Brictsi held it
from King Edward. Then it answered for 15 hides, now for 2
hides and 5 acres. Land for 6 ploughs. In lordship 2 ploughs;
10 villagers and 9 cottagers with 2 ploughs. A church; 7 slaves.
A mill at 7s; meadow, 4 acres; woodland for 40 pigs.
Value before 1066 and now £4; when acquired £3.

33 In the same manor Richard also has 5 hides. Otho held them
from King Edward. Now it answers for ½ hide.
2 villagers with 6 oxen.
1 mill at 6s.
Land for 2 ploughs.
The value is and was 20s.

In EFFINGHAM Hundred
34 In DIRTHAM* Richard holds 1½ hides. Aelmer held it from King
Edward as one manor. Salie's wife holds from Richard.
She has 1 villager and 2 smallholders.
The value was 40s; now 30s.

35 Also in DIRTHAM* are 1½ hides which Aelfric held from King Edward   35c
as one manor. Later, he gave this land to his wife and daughter,
for Chertsey church, as the men of the Hundred testify. Richard
claims* it. It does not lie in (the lands of) any manor, nor does he hold
it as a manor; but it was delivered to him. Now 3 hides* pay tax for
for 1½ hides. Land for 2 ploughs. On this land of Aelfric's, 1
plough in lordship;
2 smallholders; 2 slaves.
Value 40s.

In BLACKHEATH Hundred
36 Roger holds ALBURY from Richard. Azor held it from King Edward.
Then it answered for 4 hides, now for 2½ hides.
Land for 6 ploughs. In lordship 1;
11 villagers and 5 smallholders with 6 ploughs.
A church; 4 slaves.
A mill at 5s; woodland at 30 pigs.
Of these hides 1 man-at-arms holds 1 hide; in lordship 1½ ploughs;
1 villager and 1 slave.
Meadow, 1 acre.
Total value before 1066 £10; later 100s; now £9.

Roƀt teñ de Ricardo *SCALDEFOR* .Duo frs tenueř T.R.E.

Vñquiſq̃ habuit domũ ſuã . 7 tam manſeř in una curia.

7 quo uoluer ire potuer. Tc 7 m̃ ſe defd̃ ꝑ . IIII . hid̃ . Tra . e

VI . car . In dñio ſunt . II . car . 7 XXIX . uiłłi 7 XI . bord̃ cũ . IX.

car . Ibi æccła 7 x . ſerui . 7 III . molini de XVI . ſoł . 7 IIII . ãc

p̃ti . Silua . de xx . porc̃.   De his hid̃ teñ uñ miles

unã v̇ . ubi h̃ dim̃ car . 7 I . ſeruũ . 7 v . bord̃

Toť T.R.E. uałƀ . XVI . liƀ . 7 poſt: IX . liƀ . Modo: xx . liƀ.

Huic m̃ p̃tiñ una haga in Geldeford . de . III . ſolid̃.

Radulf teñ de Ricardo *TALEORDE*. *IN CHINGESTON HD̃*.

Edmer tenuit 7 quo uoluit ire potuit . T.R.E. Tc ſe defd̃ ꝑ.v.

hid̃ . m̃ ꝑ . II . hid̃ 7 dim̃ . Tra . e . IIII . car . In dñio . e una car.

7 VI . uiłłi 7 uñ bord̃ cũ . II . car . Ibi . II . ſerui . 7 v . ãc p̃ti.

T.R.E. 7 poſt: ualut . XL . ſoł . Modo: LX . ſoł.

Ipſe Ricard̃ teñ in dñio *TORNECROSTA*. *IN COPEDORNE HD̃*.

Cola tenuit de rege . E . Ibi ſunt m̃ in dñio . II . car . 7 v . uiłłi

7 IIII . bord̃ cũ . II . car . Ibi . IX . ſerui . 7 uñ moliñ de . XX . ſoł.

7 v . ãc p̃ti . Silua . de . I . porc̃.

Cũ iſto m̃ traditæ ſunt Ricardo iſte tre . Beceſuuorde|VI . hid̃.

Vna hid̃ 7 una v̇ quã Meruin tenebat . 7 una hida quã

teneƀ Alric 7 Almer ꝑ uno m̃ . 7 alia hida quã Coleman ^{uenator}

teneƀ ꝑ uno m̃ . Iſti hões ita libi fuer . qd̃ poterant ire

quo uolebant . 7 iſtæ træ junctæ cũ Tornecroſte . T.R.E

defdeƀ ſe ꝑ.xxv.hid̃ 7 dimid̃ . una v̇ min . Modo ꝑ . IIII.

hid̃ . IIII . ãc min . ⌐In hida quã tenuit Alric 7 Elmer.

e dim̃ car 7 II . bou in dñio . ⌐In hida Meruin . e in dñio

una car . 7 III . ãc p̃ti . ⌐In hida Coleman . ſunt . II . bord̃.

Int toť Tra . e . v . car.

37 Robert* holds SHALFORD from Richard. Two brothers held it
before 1066. Each had his own house but they remained in one court;
they could go where they would. Then and now it answered for 4 hides.
Land for 6 ploughs. In lordship 2 ploughs;
　29 villagers and 11 smallholders with 9 ploughs.
　　A church; 10 slaves.
　3 mills at 16s; meadow, 4 acres; woodland at 20 pigs.
Of these hides 1 man-at-arms holds 1 virgate,
where he has ½ plough, 1 slave and
　5 smallholders.
Total value before 1066 £16; later £9; now £20.
　1 site in Guildford belongs to this manor, at 3s.

In KINGSTON Hundred

38 Ralph holds TOLWORTH from Richard. Edmer held it; he could go
where he would before 1066. Then it answered for 5 hides, now
for 2½ hides. Land for 4 ploughs. In lordship 1 plough;
　6 villagers and 1 smallholder with 2 ploughs. 2 slaves.
　Meadow, 5 acres.
Value before 1066 and later 40s; now 60s.

In COPTHORNE Hundred

39 Richard holds THORNCROFT himself, in lordship. Cola held it
from King Edward. Now in lordship 2 ploughs;
　5 villagers and 4 smallholders with 2 ploughs. 9 slaves.
　A mill at 20s; meadow, 5 acres; woodland for 1 pig.
With this manor these lands were handed over to Richard;
Betchworth as 6 hides; 1 hide and 1 virgate which Merwin held;
1 hide which Alric and Aelmer held as 1 manor; another hide which
Colman Hunter held as 1 manor. These men were so free that they
could go where they would.
　These lands were joined with Thorncroft. Before 1066 they answered
for 25½ hides, less 1 virgate; now for 4 hides less 4 acres.
On the hide which Alric and Aelmer held, ½ plough and 2 oxen in
lordship. On Merwin's hide, 1 plough in lordship; meadow, 3 acres.
On Colman's hide, 2 smallholders. In all land for 5 ploughs.

T.R.E.ualb Tornecroſte.c.ſoł.Q̃do recep̃:ˊ lx.ſoł.Modo:ˊ
cx.ſoł.Duæ hidæ:ˊſep̃ xxx.ſoł.Hida Coleman:ˊx.ſoł.
In hoc hund̃ ten̄ʾ abb̃ de Weſtmonaſt̃.ii.hid̃.ſ; app̃ciate
In MIDEHĀ jacet.i.hida.quā tenuit ⌐in alio hund̃.
Seman de rege.E. 7 nc̄ ten̄ʾ de.W.rege. Ibi hr̃ in dn̄io
unā car̄.7 iiii.bord̃.7 dimid̃ ac̃ p̃ti.Vał 7 ualuit.xx.ſoł.
Ibid̃e ten̄ Goduiñ unā v de rege.W.Iſd̃ tenuit de
rege .Æ.Vał p ann̄.xxx.den̄.ʾ ⌐in alio hund̃.
In eod̃ HVND̄ʾ ten̄ Wiłłs fili Anſculfi.ii.hid̃.ſed app̃ciatæ S̃
35 d Oſuuold tẽ de Ricardo EPINGEHĀ. IN FINGEHĀ HVND̄.
Azor tenuit de rege.E.Tc̄ ſe deſd̃ p.vi.hid̃.Modo p.ii.
hid̃ 7 dim.Cū his.vi.hid̃ ten̄ Oſuuold.i.hid̃ 7 unā ʾv ʾtræ.
quā uñ lib̃ hō tenuit ſub rege.E.ſed p quadā neceſſitate
ſua uendidit Azori T.R.Wiłłi.Tra.ē.v.car̄ʾ int totū.
In dn̄io ſunt.ii.car̄.7 vi.uiłłi 7 v.bord̃.cū.ii.car̄.Ibi.vi.ſerui.
7 iiii.ac̃ p̃ti.7 Silua.de.v.porc̄ʾ.De herbagio:ˊiii.porc̄ʾ.
T.R.E.ualb.c.ſoł.7 poſt:ˊiiii.lib̃ 7 x.ſoł.Modo:ˊvi.lib̃.
Ipſe Ricard̃ ten̄ʾ BOCHEHĀ in dn̄io. IN WOCHINGES HVND̄ʾ.
Æłmar tenuit de rege.E.Tc̄ ſe deſd̃ p ix.hid̃.Modo p una
hida 7 dim.ʾTra.ē.ʾiiii.car̄.In dn̄io.ē una.car̄.ʾ7 vi.uiłłi
7 ii.bord̃ cū.ii.car̄.Ibi æccła.7 iii.ſerui.7 ii.æ piſcariæ de x.den̄.ʾ
7 ii.æ ac̃ p̃ti.Silua de.lx.porc̄.ʾVał 7 ualuit ſep̃.c̄ʾ.ſolid̃.

35 c, d

Value of Thorncroft before 1066, 100s; when acquired 60s; now 110s. The 2 hides,* always 30s; Colman's hide, 10s.

40* In this Hundred the Abbot of Westminster holds 2 hides, but they are assessed in another Hundred.

41* In MIDEHAM* lies 1 hide which Saeman held from King Edward. Now he holds it from King William. He has 1 plough in lordship; 3 smallholders.
Meadow, ½ acre.
The value is and was 20s.

42* There Godwin also holds 1 virgate from King William. He also held it from King Edward.
Value 30d a year.

43* In the same Hundred William son of Ansculf holds 2 hides*, but they are assessed in another Hundred.

In EFFINGHAM Hundred   35 d
44* Oswald holds EFFINGHAM from Richard. Azor held it from King Edward. Then it answered for 6 hides, now for 2½ hides. With these 6 hides Oswald holds 1 hide and 1 virgate of land which a free man held under King Edward, but he sold it to Azor for his own needs after 1066. Land for 5 ploughs in all.
In lordship 2 ploughs;
6 villagers and 5 smallholders with 2 ploughs. 6 slaves.
Meadow, 4 acres; woodland at 5 pigs; from grazing 3 pigs.
Value before 1066, 100s; later £4 10s; now £6.

In WOKING Hundred
45 Richard holds OCKHAM himself, in lordship. Aelmer held it from King Edward. Then it answered for 9 hides, now for 1½ hides. Land for 4 ploughs. In lordship 1 plough;
6 villagers and 2 smallholders with 2 ploughs.
A church; 3 slaves.
2 fisheries at 10d; meadow, 2 acres; woodland, 60 pigs.
The value is and always was 100s.

Radulf ten de Ricardo *HOCLEI*. Almar tenuit de Rege.E.

Tc 7 m̃ se defd ꝑ una hida.Tra.ē.IIII.car.In dñio.ē una.7 IX uilli
7 III.borđ cũ.IIII.car.Silua de.xx.porc.7 II.serui.

T.R.E.ualb.lxx.solid.7 post 7 modo: similiter.

Ibi hoc m̃ ten ipse Ricarđ dim̃ hida.Aluuiñ tenuit.T.R.E.7 po
tuit cũ ea ire quo uoluit.Tc ꝑ dim̃ hida.m̃ ꝑ nichilo.In Hoclei apꝑciat.

Ipse Ricarđ ten in dñio *BECESWORDE*. *IN WODETONE HVND.*

Cola tenuit de rege.E.Tc se defd ꝑ.VI.hiđ 7 m̃ ꝑ.II.hiđ.Tra.ē
VII.car.In dñio ē una car.7 VI.uilti 7 x.borđ cũ.III.car.Ibi.VI.serui.
7 uñ moliñ de.x.sol.7 III.ac ꝑti.Silua de qt xx.porc.De herbag.VI.porc.

Ibi æccta.T.R.E.7 post: IX.lib.Modo: VIII.lib.

Ipse Ricarđ ten *ARSESTE*.Almar tenuit de rege.E.Tc 7 m̃
se defd ꝑ.II.hiđ.Tra.ē.IIII.car.Ibi sunt.VIII.uilli cũ.III.car.
Silua de.xv.porc.   T.R.E.7 post 7 m̃: ual.xlv.solid.

H tra fuit cujdã libi hõis.7 potuit cũ ea ire quo libuit.nec ptiñ ulli m̃

                                        ſRicardi.

.XX.

TERRA WILLI DE BRAIOSE. *IN COPEDEDORNE HVND.*

Witts de Braiose ten 7 Halsart de eo *TADORNE*.Godtoui
tenuit de Heraldo.7 potuit ire quo uoluit.Tc se defd ꝑ.v.hiđ.m̃
ꝑ dim̃ hida.Tra.ē.III.car.In dñio.ē una car.7 II.uilti 7 v.borđ
cũ una car.Silua: de.III.porc.T.R.E.ual.c.sol.7 post: xx.M: xlv.

Halsard ten de Witto *BOCHEHÃ*.Godtoui *IN FINGEHÃ HVND.*
tenuit de Heraldo.Tc se defd ꝑ.v.hiđ.m̃ ꝑ.II.hiđ.Tra.ē.III.car.
In dñio.ē una.7 III.uilti 7 IIII.borđ.cũ.I.car.Ibi.IIII.ac ꝑti.De pas
nagio 7 herbagio: xi.porc.T.R.E.7 post: ualuit.l.sol.Modo: lx.sol.

[In WOTTON Hundred] *

46 Ralph holds OCKLEY from Richard. Aelmer held it from King
Edward. Then and now it answered for 1 hide. Land for 4 ploughs.
In lordship 1;
    9 villagers and 3 smallholders with 4 ploughs.
    Woodland at 20 pigs; 2 slaves.
Value before 1066, 70s; later and now the same.
    In this manor Richard holds ½ hide* himself. Alwin held it
before 1066; he could go with it where he would. Then
for ½ hide, now for nothing. It is assessed in Ockley.

47 Richard holds BETCHWORTH himself, in lordship. Cola held it from
King Edward. Then it answered for 6 hides, now for 2 hides.
Land for 7 ploughs. In lordship 1 plough;
    6 villagers and 10 smallholders with 3 ploughs. 6 slaves.
    A mill at 10s; meadow, 3 acres; woodland at 80 pigs;
        from grazing, 6 pigs. A church.
Before 1066 and later £9; now £8.

48 Richard holds HARTSHURST himself. Aelmer held it from King Edward.
Then and now it answered for 2 hides. Land for 4 ploughs.
    8 villagers with 3 ploughs.
    Woodland at 15 pigs.
Value before 1066, later and now 45s.
    This land was a free man's; he could go with it where
he would. It does not belong to any of Richard's manors.

20   LAND OF WILLIAM OF BRAOSE

In COPTHORNE Hundred
1 William of Braose holds TADWORTH, and Halsard from him. Godtovi
held it from Earl Harold; he could go where he would. Then it
answered for 5 hides, now for ½ hide. Land for 3 ploughs. In
lordship 1 plough.
    2 villagers and 5 smallholders with 1 plough.
    Woodland at 3 pigs.
Value before 1066, 100s; later 20s; now 45s.

In EFFINGHAM Hundred
2 Halsard holds (Little) BOOKHAM from William. Godtovi held it from
Earl Harold. Then it answered for 5 hides, now for 2 hides.
Land for 3 ploughs. In lordship 1;
    3 villagers and 4 smallholders with 1 plough.
    Meadow, 4 acres; from pasturage and grazing, 11 pigs.
Value before 1066 and later 50s; now 60s.

TERRA WILLI FILIJ ANSCVLFI. *IN WALETONE HVND.*

Witts fili Anſculfi ten *WITFORD* . 7 Witts de eo. Lanch tenuit
tenuit de rege. E. Tc ſe defd p. 11. hid. M p una hida. Tra. e
In dnio. e una car. 7 11. uitti cu. 1. car. 7 un molin de xx. ſot. 7 xxiiii.
ac pti. T.R.E. uatb. L. ſot. 7 poſt. xxii. ſot. Modo. LX. ſolid.

Iſde Witts ten *MICHELHA.* Lemar tenuit de rege. E. Tc 7 m
ſe defd p. 11. hid 7 una v. Ibi ſunt. 11. uitti 7 vi. cot. 7 dim molin
de. xx. ſot. T.R.E. 7 m uat. xL. ſot. Cu recep. xiii. ſot 7 iiii. den.

Ipſe Witts ten *WENDELESORDE.* *IN BRIXISTAN HVND.*
Sex ſochi tenuer de rege. E. 7 potuer ire quo uoluer. Ibi eran. 11. hallæ.

36 a Tc 7 m ſe defd p. xii. hid. Tra. e. iiii. car. Hanc tra habuit
Anſculf poſtq recep uicecomitatu. ſed hoes de hund dnt ſe
non uidiſſe ſigillu nec libatore.

Ansfrid. v. hid. m p una hida. Heldred. iii. hid. m p nichilo.
Vluuard. iii. hid. Walter. i. hid. Ñ ded geld.
In tra iſtoz ſunt. 11. car in dnio. 7 dim. 7 v. uitti 7 xxii. bord
cu. 11. car. 7 xxii. ac pti. Tot M. T.R.E. uatb. cx. ſot. 7 poſt.
L. ſot. Modo. viii. lib. int totu. *IN WODETONE HVND.*

Balduin ten de ipſo Witto *MILDETONE.* Vluric tenuit
de rege. E. Tc ſe defd p. vi. hid. modo p. iiii. hid 7 dim. Tra. e
v. car. In dnio. e. 1. car. 7 x. uitti 7 ix. bord. cu. iiii. car. 7 iiii.
ſerui. 7 un molin de. 11. ſot. 7 11. ac pti. Silua de. ix. porc. De
herbag. x. porc. T.R.E. uatb. Lxx. ſot. 7 poſt. 7 modo. LX. ſot.
In *HVND* Copededorne ſunt. 11. hidæ. quæ ptin huic M. Vat. xx. ſot.

In WALLINGTON Hundred
1 William son of Ansculf holds WHITFORD*, and William the Chamberlain
from him. Lank held it from King Edward. Then it answered for
2 hides, now for 1 hide. Land for .... In lordship 1 plough.
  2 villagers with 1 plough.
  1 mill at 20s; meadow, 24 acres.
Value before 1066, 50s; later 22s; now 60s.

2 William also holds MITCHAM. Ledmer*held it from King Edward.
Then and now it answered for 2 hides and 1 virgate.
  2 villagers and 6 cottagers.
  ½ mill at 20s.
Value before 1066 and now 40s; when acquired 13s 4d.

In BRIXTON Hundred
3 William holds WANDSWORTH himself. 6 Freemen held it from King
Edward; they could go where they would. There were two Halls.
Then and now it answered for 12 hides. Land for 4 ploughs.   36a
Ansculf had this land after he received the Sheriffdom, but the men
of the Hundred say that they have seen neither seal or a deliverer.
  Ansfrid 5 hides, now for 1 hide; Heldred*, 3 hides, now for
nothing; Wulfward, 3 hides; Walter the Vinedresser, 1 hide;
they did not pay tax. On their lands, 2½ ploughs in lordship;
  5 villagers and 22 smallholders with 2 ploughs.
  Meadow, 22 acres.
Value of the whole manor before 1066, 110s; later 50s; now £8 in all.

In WOTTON Hundred
4 Baldwin holds MILTON from William himself. Wulfric held it from
King Edward. Then it answered for 6 hides, now for 4½ hides.
Land for 5 ploughs. In lordship 1 plough;
  10 villagers and 9 smallholders with 4 ploughs; 4 slaves.
  A mill at 2s; meadow, 2 acres; woodland at 9 pigs;
    from grazing, 10 pigs.
Value before 1066, 70s; later and now 60s.
  In Copthorne Hundred are 2 hides which belong to this manor.*
Value 20s.

Isdē Balduin ten de Witto . I . hidā ad Hanſtega . Ordui te
nuit . 7 dim hid ten Balduin ad Litelfeld . Alfer tenuit . Hi duo
potuer ire quo uoluer . cū tris ſuis . Ibi . I . car . ē in dñio . cū uno
bord . Val . xi . ſol 7 III . den.

Ipſe Witts ten *ABINCEBORNE* . Huſcarle tenuit de rege . E.
Tc ſe defd ꝑ . vi . hid . m̄ ꝑ . IIII . hid . Tra . ē . IX . car . In dñio ſuꝗ
.II . car . 7 x . uitti 7 vii . bord cū . v . car . | 7 v . ſerui . 7 uñ moliñ *Ibi æccla.*
de . vi . ſol . 7 III . ac̄ p̄ti . De herbagio 7 paſnagio . xl . porc̄.
T . R . E . ualb . viii . lib . 7 poſt . 7 modo . vii . lib.

Ipſe Witts ten *PADENDENE* . Huſcarle tenuit de rege . E.
Tc ſe defd ꝑ . IIII . hid . Modo ꝑ . III , hid . Tra . ē . IX . car . In dñio nil . ē.
ſed ibi . XII . uitti 7 v . bord . cū . vi . car . 7 uñ moliñ de . vi . ſolid.
7 IIII . ac̄ p̄ti . Silua . xl . porc̄ . de herbag . xv . porc̄.
De hoc M̄ ten Hugo hō Witti . III . hid cū halla . 7 in dñio . I . car̄.
Tot M̄ T . R . E . ualb . viiii . lib . 7 poſt . vii . lib . Modo . ſimilit . vii . lb.

.XX.
.II.

TERRA WALTERIJ FILIJ OTHER. *IN GODELMINGE HVND.*
WALTERI filius Otheri ten *CONTONE* . Brixi tenuit de rege
. E . Tc ſe defd ꝑ . xiiii . hid . modo ꝑ . xi . hid . Tra . ē . x . car . In dñio
ſunt . III . car . 7 xxi . uitts 7 viii . cot cū . vi . car . Ibi . vii . ſerui.
7 vii . ac̄ p̄ti . Ibi eccla . T . R . E . ualb . viii . lib . 7 poſt . vi . lib . Modo . ix . lib.
Tezelin ten de Walterio *HORMERA* . Aluuin tenuit de rege
. Ed . Tc ſe defd ꝑ . xv . hid . modo ꝑ . III . hid . Tra . ē . III . car . In dñio
ſunt . II . car . 7 III . uitti 7 II . cot cū . I . car 7 dim . Ibi . I . moliñ de . xi.
ſol . 7 vi . ac̄ p̄ti . T . R . E . ualb . l . ſol . Poſt . xxx . ſol . Modo . c . ſolid.

5 Baldwin also holds 1 hide at ANSTIE from William; Ordwy held it.
Baldwin holds ½ hide at 'LITTLEFIELD'; Alfhere held it.
These two could go where they would with their lands.
In lordship 1 plough, with
  1 smallholder.
Value 11s 3d.

6 William holds ABINGER himself. Guard* held it from King Edward.
Then it answered for 6 hides, now for 4 hides. Land for 9 ploughs.
In lordship 2 ploughs;
  10 villagers and 7 smallholders with 5 ploughs.
    A church, 5 slaves.
    A mill at 6s; meadow, 3 acres; from grazing and pasture, 40 pigs.
Value before 1066 £8; later and now £7.

7 William holds PADDINGTON himself. Guard* held it from King
Edward. Then it answered for 4 hides, now for 3 hides.
Land for 9 ploughs. Nothing in lordship. But there are
  12 villagers and 5 smallholders with 6 ploughs.
  A mill at 6s; meadow, 4 acres; woodland, 40 pigs;
    from grazing, 15 pigs.
  Hugh, William's man, holds 3 hides of this manor,
  with the Hall. In lordship 1 plough.
Value of the whole manor before 1066 £9; later £7; now the same, £7.

22   LAND OF WALTER SON OF OTHERE

In GODALMING Hundred
1 Walter son of Othere holds COMPTON. Brictsi held it from King
Edward. Then it answered for 14 hides, now for 11 hides. Land
for 10 ploughs. In lordship 3 ploughs;
  21 villagers* and 8 cottagers with 6 ploughs. 7 slaves.
  Meadow, 7 acres. A church.
Value before 1066 £8; later £6; now £9.

2 Tesselin holds HURTMORE from Walter. Alwin held it from King
Edward. Then it answered for 15 hides, now for 3 hides.
Land for 3 ploughs. In lordship 2 ploughs;
  3 villagers and 2 cottagers with 1½ ploughs.
  1 mill at 11s; meadow, 6 acres.
Value before 1066, 50s; later 30s; now 100s.

Ipſe Walteri⁹ 7 Girardus de eo teñ *PIPEREHERGE* . Aluuard
tenuit de rege . E . Tc ſe defd ꝑ . v . hid . Modo ꝑ . iii . hid . Tra . e
iii . car . In dño ſunt . ii . car . 7 uñ moliñ de xv . ſot . 7 vii . ac ꝑti.
Ibi . iiii . uiłłi 7 iii . cot cu . i . car . T . R . E . 7 poſt :̃ ualb . xxx . ſot . M :̃ c . ſot.
Ipſe Walterius teñ unu hoem de ſoca de *IN CHINGEST HD.*
chingeſtun . cui comendau eq̃s ſiluaticas regis cuſtodire . ſ; neſcim
quom . Hic ho teñ . ii . hid . ſed ñ ht rectu in ipſa tra . ꝑ . ii . hid
ſe defdb . m̃ ꝑ nichilo . Ibi . e in dño . i . car . cu . iii . ſeruis . 7 i . piſcaria
de . cxxv . anguiłł . 7 una ac ꝑti . Vat 7 ualuit ſep xxx . ſot . ✿

.XXII

WALTERI⁹ De Doai teñ *IN WALETON HD.* TERRA WALT DE DOWAI.
. ii . hid de rege . ſic dicit . S; hoes de hund dut ſe nunq̃ uidiſſe breue
ł nunciu regis q̃ eu inde ſaiſiſſet . Hoc aut teſtant . qd quida lib ho
hanc tra teneꝗ 7 quo uellet abire ualeꝗ . ſumiſit ſe in manu Waltij
ꝑ defenſione ſui . H tra uat 7 ualuit . xx . ſot.

36 b .XXII.   TERRA GISLEBTI FILIJ RICHERIJ.
GISLEBERT⁹ fili⁹ Richerii
de Aigle teñ *WITLEI* . Goduin tenuit . Tc ſe defd ꝑ xx . hid . Modo
ꝑ xii . hid . Tra . e . xvi . car . In dño ſunt . ii . car . 7 xxxvii . uiłłi 7 iii . cot.
cu xiii . car . Ibi æccła . 7 iii . ac prati . Silua . de xxx . porc.
T . R . E . 7 poſt . ualb . xv . lib . Modo :̃ xvi . lib

3 Walter holds PEPER HARROW himself and Gerard from him. Alfward
   held it from King Edward. Then it answered for 5 hides, now
   for 3 hides. Land for 3 ploughs. In lordship 2 ploughs.
     A mill at 15s; meadow, 7 acres.
     4 villagers and 3 cottagers with 1 plough.
   Value before 1066 and later 30s; now 100s.

In KINGSTON Hundred
4 Walter himself holds 1 man of the Jurisdiction of Kingston to whom he
   has assigned the charge of the King's forest mares, but we do
   not know how. This man holds 2 hides, but he has no right
   in that land. It answered for 2 hides, now for nothing.
   In lordship 1 plough, with
     3 slaves.
     1 fishery of 125 eels; meadow, 1 acre.
   The value is and always was 30s.

Ø *(5 is misplaced, before chapter 27, in col. 36 b, with transposition signs)*

23* LAND OF WALTER OF DOUAI

In WALLINGTON Hundred
1 Walter of Douai holds 2 hides from the King. So he states, but the
   men of the Hundred state that they have never seen the King's writ or an
   emissary who put him in possession of it. However they testify
   that a free man who held this land, and was able to go where
   he would, put himself in Walter's hands for his own protection.
   The value of this land is and was 20s.

24* LAND OF GILBERT SON OF RICHERE   36b

[In GODALMING Hundred] *
1 Gilbert son of Richere of L'Aigle holds WITLEY. Earl Godwin
   held it. Then it answered for 20 hides, now for 12 hides.
   Land for 16 ploughs. In lordship 2 ploughs;
     37 villagers and 3 cottagers with 13 ploughs. A church.
     Meadow, 3 acres; woodland at 30 pigs.
   Value before 1066 and later £15; now £16.

GOISFRID de Manneuile ten *CLOPEHA*. Turbern tenuit
de rege. E. Tc se defd. p. x. hid. modo p. III. hid. Tra. e
VII. car. In dnio. e una car. 7 VIII. uilli 7 III. bord cu. v. car.
Ibi. v. ac pti. T.R.E. ualb x. lib. Post. similit. Modo. VII. lib 7 x. sol.
Dnt hoes qd Goisfrid hoc M injuste ht. qa ad tra Asgari
n ptinet. Qd Goisfrid de hoc M p elemosina dedit. ual xx. sol.
Ipse Goisfrid ten *AVLTONE*. Quinq *IN WALETON HVND*.
libi hoes de rege. E. 7 poteraī ire quo uolebaī. Hoꝝ un
teneb. II. hid. 7 quattuor unquisq. VI. hid. Quinq M fuer.
Modo. e in unu. M. Tc se defd p. xxVII. hid. Modo p. III. hid
7 dim. Tra. e. x. car. In dnio. e una. 7 IX. uilli 7 IX. cot cu
.v. car. Ibi æccla 7 VII. serui. 7 XII. ac pti.
Hoes de comitatu 7 de hund dnt nunq se uidisse breue
uel libatore qui ex parte regis Goisfrid de hoc M saisisset.
T.R.E. ualb. xx. lib. Qdo saisiuit. c. sol. Modo. x. lib.
De his hid ten Wesman. VI. hid. de Goisfrido filio Eustachij.
hanc tra ded ei Goisfrid cu filia sua. In dnio. e. I. car. 7 III.
uilli 7 un cot cu. III. car. 7 un molin de. xxxv. solid. 7 III.
serui. 7 x. ac pti. Silua. de. II. porc. Tra. e. II. car.
T.R.E. ualb. IIII. lib. 7 post. xL. sol. Modo. cx. sol.
De eisd hid ht qda faber regis dim hid. qua T.R.E. accep
cu uxore sua. sed nunq inde seruitiu fecit. *IN WOCHINGES HD.*
Ipse Goisfrid ten *WENEBERGE*. Non. e de tra Asgar.
Suen 7 Leuuin tenuer de rege. E. Tc se defd p. VII. hid.
Modo p. III. hid. Tra. e. VII. car. Duo M fuer. modo. e un.
In dnio. e una car. 7 XII. uilli 7 xVII. bord cu. VIII. car.
Ibi æccla 7 VIII. serui. 7 VI. ac pti. Silua. de xxx. porc.
Tot T.R.E. ualb VII. lib. Post. c. sol. Modo. VII. lib.

.XXVI.
GOISFRID Orlatele
ten' BELGEHAM
sine dono regis. 7 sine
Warant. Anschil te
nuit de Heraldo. Tc se
defd p. v. hid. modo
p nichilo. Tra. e. II. car'.
In dnio. e una. 7 I. uills
7 un bord cu dim' car.
Ibi un' seru'. 7 VIII. ac pti.
T.R.E. ualb. vI. lib. Post.'
xx. sol. Modo. xl. sol.

In BRIXTON Hundred
1 Geoffrey de Mandeville holds CLAPHAM. Thorbern held it from
King Edward. Then it answered for 10 hides, now for 3 hides.
Land for 7 ploughs. In lordship 1 plough;
   8 villagers and 3 smallholders with 5 ploughs.
   Meadow, 5 acres.
Value before 1066 £10; later the same; now £7 10s.
   The men (of the Hundred) state that Geoffrey has this manor
   wrongfully because it does* not belong to Asgar's* land.
Value of what Geoffrey gave in alms from this manor, 20s.

In WALLINGTON Hundred
2 Geoffrey holds CARSHALTON himself. 5 free men (held it) from
King Edward; they could go where they would. One of them held
2 hides, and four 6 hides each. There were five manors;
now it is in one manor. Then it answered for 27* hides,
now for 3½ hides. Land for 10 ploughs. In lordship 1;
   9 villagers and 9 cottagers with 5 ploughs. A church; 7 slaves.
   Meadow, 12 acres.
   The men of the County and of the Hundred state that they have
   never seen a writ or a deliverer who put Geoffrey in possession
   of this manor on the King's behalf.
Value before 1066 £20; when he took possession 100s; now £10.
   Wesman holds 6 of these hides from Geoffrey son of Count
   Eustace; to whom Geoffrey de Mandeville gave this land, with
   his daughter. In lordship 1 plough;
   3 villagers and 1 cottager with 3 ploughs.
   A mill at 35s; 3 slaves; meadow, 10 acres; woodland at 2 pigs.
   Land for 2 ploughs.
Value before 1066 £4; later 40s; now 110s.
   Of these hides one of the King's smiths has ½ hide, which he
   received with his wife before 1066; but he has never done service for it.

In WOKING Hundred
3 Geoffrey holds WANBOROUGH himself. It is not (part) of Asgar's
land. Swein and Leofwin, brothers,* held it from King Edward.
Then it answered for 7 hides, now for 3 hides. Land for 7 ploughs.
There were two manors; now it is one. In lordship 1 plough;
   12 villagers and 17 smallholders with 8 ploughs.
      A church; 8 slaves.
   Meadow, 6 acres; woodland at 30 pigs.
Total value before 1066 £7; later 100s; now £7.

IN *WOCHINGES* HD.

❀ Walteri fili Otheri ten ORSELEI. Brixi tenuit de rege . E.

Tc se defd p . x . hid . Modo p . viii . hid . Tra . e . vi . car . In dnio

sunt . ii . car . 7 xiiii . uilli 7 v . bord cu . v . car . Ibi æccla

7 viii . serui . Silua de . xx . porc.

T . R . E . ualb . viii . lib . Post : c . sol . Modo : vi . lib . ⨍ Val . xx . sol.

De hac tra ten un Anglic . i . hid . 7 ibi ht . i . car . cu . i . bord.

.XXVI

TERRA EDWARDI SARISBER IN *AMELEBRIGE* HD.

EDWARD Sarisbiensis ten *WALETONE* . Azor tenuit

de rege . E . Tc se defd p . vi . hid . Modo p . iii . hid . Tra . e . viii .

car . In dnio sunt . ii . car . 7 viii . uilli 7 iii . cot cu . vii . car.

Ibi . viii . serui . 7 un molin de xii . sol . 7 vi . den . 7 xl . ac pti.

Silua de . l . porc . Ibi un forestari de . x . sol.   ⨍ xiiii . lib

T . R . E . ualb . viii . lib . Post : c . solid . Modo : xii . lib . Tam redd

Rannulf ten de Edwardo *HAMELEDONE* . IN *GODELMINGE* HD.

Azor tenuit de rege . E . Tc se defd p . v . hid . Modo p . iii . hid.

Tra . e . iiii . car . In dnio sunt . ii . car . 7 viii . uilli 7 un cot cu . v . car.

Ibi . xiii . serui . 7 un molin de . xxx . den . 7 iii . ac pti . Silua : xxx . porc.

Hugo IN *WOCHINGES* HVND . ⨍ Val 7 ualuit sep . c . solid.

ten de Edwardo *CLANEDVN* . Fulcui tenuit . T . R . E . Tc se defd ☞

36 b

26*   [LAND OF GEOFFREY ORLATEILE]

[In BRIXTON Hundred]

1 Geoffrey Orlateile holds BALHAM, without the King's gift or warrant.
Askell held it from Earl Harold. Then it answered for 5 hides,
now for nothing. Land for 2 ploughs. In lordship 1;
    1 villager and 1 smallholder with ½ plough. 1 slave.
    Meadow, 8 acres.
Value before 1066 £6; later 20s; now 40s.

22

In WOKING Hundred

5* Walter son of Othere holds (West) HORSLEY. Brictsi held it from
King Edward. Then it answered for 10 hides, now for 8 hides.
Land for 6 ploughs. In lordship 2 ploughs;
    14 villagers and 5 smallholders with 5 ploughs.
    A church; 8 slaves.
    Woodland, 20 pigs.
Value before 1066 £8; later 100s; now £6.
    An Englishman holds 1 hide of this land. He has 1 plough there,
with 1 smallholder. Value 20s.

27   LAND OF EDWARD OF SALISBURY

In ELMBRIDGE Hundred

1 Edward of Salisbury holds WALTON (-on-Thames). Azor held it from
King Edward. Then it answered for 6 hides, now for 3 hides.
Land for 8 ploughs. In lordship 2 ploughs;
    8 villagers and 3 cottagers with 7 ploughs. 8 slaves.
    A mill at 12s 6d; meadow, 40 acres; woodland at 50 pigs;
    1 forester, at 10s.
Value before 1066 £8; later 100s; now £12; however, it pays £14.

In GODALMING Hundred

2 Ranulf holds HAMBLEDON from Edward. Azor held it from King
Edward. Then it answered for 5 hides, now for 3 hides.
Land for 4 ploughs. In lordship 2 ploughs;
    8 villagers and 1 cottager with 5 ploughs. 13 slaves.
    A mill at 30d; meadow, 3 acres; woodland, 30 pigs.
The value is and always was 100s.

In WOKING Hundred

3 Hugh holds (West) CLANDON from Edward. Fulk held it before 1066.
Then it answered* for 5 hides, now for 2½ hides. Land for 3 ploughs.

☞ ⌐p.v.hiđ.Modo ⌐p.ii.hiđ 7 dimidia.Tra.ē.iii.cař.In dñio.ē una.7 iiii.uilli
7 v.borđ.cū.i.car 7 dim̃.Moliñ de.iii.fot.Ibi æccła.7 Silua.de.v.porc.
⌐Valuit.L.fot.Modo.LX.fot.

36 c
TERRA ROBERTI MALET. *In Wichinges hđ.*

.XXVI. Rotbertvs Malet ten *Svdtvne*. Wenefi tenuit de
rege.E.Tc̄ fe defđ ⌐p.v.hiđ.Modo ⌐p.iii.hiđ.Tra.ē.iii.cař.
In dñio.ē una.7 v.uilłi 7 v.borđ cū.ii.cař.Ibi.vi.ferui.
7 uñ moliñ de.v.foliđ.7 xx.āc p̃ti.Silua.de.xxv.porc.
T.R.E.7 poſt.ualuit.viii.liƀ.Modo.c.foliđ.
Hanc trā faifiuit Durand 7 dñt hōes qđ injuſte h̃.nā
nemo eoꝛ breuē regis uel libatorē uidit.

TERRA MILONIS CRISPIN *In Waletone hđ.*

.XXIX. Milo Crefpin ten *Beddintone*.7 Wiłłs fił Turoldi de eo.
Vlf tenuit de rege.E.Tc̄ fe defđ ⌐p.xxv.hiđ.Modo ⌐p.iii.
hiđ.Tra.ē.vi.cař.In dñio.ē una cař.7 xiii.uilłi 7 xiii.
cot cū.vi.cař.Ibi uñ feruus.7 ii.molini de xxx.v.fot.
7 xx.āc p̃ti.Silua de.v.porc.
T.R.E.uałƀ.x.liƀ.Poſt.vi.liƀ.Modo.ix.liƀ 7 x.fot.
De iſto M̄ ablatæ fuꝑ xxi.mafur q̃s Rogeri ten.
In Lundon.xiii.In Sudwerche.viii.Redđt.xii.foliđ
Ipfe Milo ten *Cisedvne*.Magno *In Chingest hđ.*
tenuit T.R.E.Tc̄ fe defđ ⌐p.v.hiđ modo ⌐p una hida.
Q̃do rex.W.uenit in Anglia.Wigot ñ habeƀ.Tra.ē
iii.cař.In Beddinton jaceƀ h̃ tra.Viłłi teneƀ.In dñio
ē m̃ una cař.7 vi.uilłi cū.ii.cař.
T.R.E.uałƀ.iiii.liƀ Poſt.xL.fot.Modo.LXX.foliđ.

In lordship 1;
  4 villagers and 5 smallholders with 1½ ploughs.
  A mill at 3s. A church; woodland at 5 pigs*.
The value was 50s; now 60s.*

28   **LAND OF ROBERT MALET**

In WOKING Hundred
1 Robert Malet holds SUTTON (-by-Guildford). Wynsi held it
  from King Edward. Then it answered for 5 hides, now for 3 hides.
  Land for 3 ploughs. In lordship 1;
    5 villagers and 5 smallholders with 2 ploughs. 6 slaves.
    A mill at 5s; meadow, 20 acres; woodland at 25 pigs.
  Value before 1066 and later £8; now 100s.
    Durand took possession of this land, and the men (of the Hundred)
  state that he has it wrongfully, for none of them has seen the King's
  writ or a deliverer.

29   **LAND OF MILES CRISPIN**

In WALLINGTON Hundred
1 Miles Crispin holds BEDDINGTON, and William son of Thorold from him.
  Wulf held it from King Edward. Then it answered for 25 hides,
  now for 3 hides. Land for 6 ploughs. In lordship 1 plough;
    13 villagers and 13 cottagers with 6 ploughs. 1 slave.
    2 mills at 35s; meadow, 20 acres; woodland at 5 pigs.
  Value before 1066 £10; later £6; now £9 10s.
    21 dwellings, which Earl Roger holds, have been taken from this
  manor*; 13 in London, 8 in Southwark. They pay 12s.

In KINGSTON Hundred
2 Miles holds CHESSINGTON* himself. Magnus Swarthy held it
  before 1066. Then it answered for 5 hides, now for 1 hide.
  When King William came to England Wigot* did not have it.
  Land for 3 ploughs. This land lay in (the lands of) Beddington.
  The villagers held it. Now in lordship 1 plough;
    6 villagers with 2 ploughs.
  Value before 1066 £4; later 40s; now 70s.

XXX

TERRA HAIMONIS VICECOMIT. *IN TENRIGE HD.*

Haimo uicecom ten *TICESEI*. Goltoui tenuit de rege. E.

Tc se defd .p. xx. hid. Modo .p. ii. hid. Tra. ē. viii. car.

In dnio sunt. iiii. car. 7 xiiii. uitti 7 xxxi. bord cū. v.

car. Ibi æccta 7 ix. serui. .p pastura septim porc uittoʒ.

T. R. E. uatb. x. lib. Post. vi. lib. Modo. xi. lib.

Ipse Haimo ten *CABREWELLE*. *IN BRIXISTAN HD*

Norman tenuit de rege. E. Tc se defd .p xii. hid. Modo

.p vi. hid 7 una v. Tra. ē. v. car. In dnio sunt. ii. 7 xxii. uitti

7 vii. bord cū. vi. car. Ibi æccta. 7 lxiii. ac pti. Silua. de lx.

porc.　　　　T. R. E. uatb. xii. lib. Post. vi. lib. Modo. xii. lib.

XXXI

TERRA HVNFRIDI CAMERAR *IN CHINGESTVN HD.*

Hvnfrid camerar ten de feuo reginæ *CVBE*. Alured tenuit de

rege. 7 poterat ire quo uoleb. Tc se defd .p iii. hid. m̄ .p nichilo.

Tra. ē. ii. car. In dnio. ē una. 7 iii. uitti 7 iiii. bord cū una car.

Ibi. viii. ac pti. T. R. E. uatb. iiii. lib. Post. xx. sot. Modo. c. sot.

T. R. W. femina quæ hanc trā teneb misit se cū ea in manu reginæ.

TERRA RADVLFI DE FELGERES. *IN COPEDEDORNE HD.*

Radvlfvs De Felgeres ten *HALLEGA*. Goda comitissa tenuit de

rege. E. Tc se defd .p. vii. hid. m̄ .p. ii. hid 7 una v. Tra. ē

In dnio. ē. i. car. 7 ix. uitti 7 v. bord. cū. v. car. Ibi. viii. serui.

Silua. de. xv. porc. T. R. E. uatb. vii. lib. Post 7 m̄. c. solid.

30   LAND OF HAMO THE SHERIFF

In TANDRIDGE Hundred

1 Hamo the Sheriff holds TITSEY. Godtovi* held it from King
   Edward. Then it answered for 20 hides, now for 2 hides.
   Land for 8 ploughs. In lordship 4 ploughs;
      14 villagers and 31 smallholders with 5 ploughs. A church;
      9 slaves.
   For pasture, the villagers' seventh pig.*
   Value before 1066 £10; later £6; now £11.

In BRIXTON Hundred

2 Hamo holds CAMBERWELL himself. Norman held it from King Edward.
   Then it answered for 12 hides, now for 6 hides and 1 virgate.
   Land for 5 ploughs. In lordship 2;
      22 villagers and 7 smallholders with 6 ploughs. A church.
   Meadow, 63 acres; woodland at 60 pigs.
   Value before 1066 £12; later £6; now £14.

31   LAND OF HUMPHREY THE CHAMBERLAIN

In KINGSTON Hundred

1 Humphrey the Chamberlain holds COOMBE from the Queen's holding.
   Alfred held it from King [Edward] *; he could go where he would.
   Then it answered for 3 hides, now for nothing.
   Land for 2 ploughs. In lordship 1;
      3 villagers and 4 smallholders with 1 plough.
   Meadow, 8 acres.
   Value before 1066 £4; later 20s; now 100s.
   After 1066 the woman who held this land put herself in the
   Queen's hands with it.

32   LAND OF RALPH OF FEUGERES

In COPTHORNE Hundred

1 Ralph of Feugeres holds HEADLEY. Countess Goda held it
   from King Edward. Then it answered for 7 hides, now for 2 hides
   and 1 virgate. Land for .... In lordship 1 plough;
      9 villagers and 5 smallholders with 5 ploughs. 8 slaves.
   Woodland at 15 pigs.
   Value before 1066 £7; later and now 100s.

Ipſe Radulf⁹ʰ teñ *WESCOTE* . Alſi abƀ *IN WODETON HD*.

tenuit de rege . E . Tc̄ ſe defđ ⱷ x . hiđ . Modo ⱷ . iii . hiđ.

Tʰra . ē . vii . caʰr . In dñio . ē una caʰr . 7 xiiii . uiħi 7 v . borđ

cū . vii . caʰr . Ibi . iii . ſerui . 7 uñ moliñ de . xxx . denaʰr . 7 ii . ac̄ p̄ti.

7 dim . Silua . de xxx . porc̄ . T . R . E . uaɫƀ . ix . liƀ . Poſt 7 m̄ʰ viii . liƀ.

.XXX.ⁱⁱⁱ

36 d ## TERRA ALVREDI DE MEʰRLEƀ *IN WOCHINGES HD*

ALVREDVS teñ de rege *SANDE* . 7 Rainaldus de eo.

Carlo tɔneƀ T . R . E . Tc̄ 7 m̄ ſe defenđ ⱷ . xx . hiɫ.

Tʰra . x . caʰr . In dñio ſt̄ . ii . caʰr . 7 viii . ſerui . 7 xiiii . uiħi

7 x . borđ cū . vi . caʰr . Ibi moliñ redđ . xxi . ſoɫ 7 vi . denaʰr.

Ibi æccɫa . 7 v . piſcariæ redđ . liiii . denaʰr . 7 c . ac̄ p̄ti . xvi . min⁹.

Silua de . c . lx . porc̄.

De hac ʰtra teñ Walter⁹ . i . hiđ 7 dimʰ . 7 Herƀt⁹ . ix . de ʰtra uiħoʒ.

Ibi ſt̄ in dñio . ii . caʰr . 7 vii . ſerui . 7 uñ⁹ uiħs . 7 xvi . borđ.

Ibi moliñ redđ . ii . ſoɫ.

Tot̄ T . R . E . uaɫƀ . xx . liƀ . Modo dñiū . x . liƀ . 7 aliud . cx . ſoliđ.

.XXXII.ⁱⁱ

TERRA ALBERTI. *IN WALETON HVND.*

ALBERTVS cleric̄ teñ⁹ de rege *EDDINTONE* . Oſuuard teneƀ de rege . E.

Tc̄ ſe defđ ⱷ . viii . hiđ . Modo ⱷ . iiᵃᵇ⁷ . Tʰra . iiii . caʰr . In dñio ſt̄ . ii . caʰr.

7 v . uiħi 7 iiii . cot ᵉcū . i . caʰr 7 dimiđ . Silua . xx . porc̄ʰ.

T . R . E . 7 modo . c . ſoliđ.

.XXXV.

TERRA ODARDI. *IN AMELEBRIGE HVND.*

ODARD⁹ baliſtari⁹ teñ⁹ de rege . iiii . hiđ in Aiſſela . Toui tenuit de

rege . E . Nc̄ ſe defđ ⱷ una hiđ . Ibi ſunt . x . uiħi cū . ii . caʰr . 7 ii . ac̄ p̄ti.

Idē Odard⁹ teñʰ *MOLESHA* . Toui tenuit de rege . E. ⌐ Vaɫ xl . ſoɫ.

Tc̄ ſe defđ ⱷ . vi . hiđ 7 una v̄ . Modo ⱷ una hida . Tʰra . ē . iii . caʰrʰ . In dñio

ē una . 7 x . uiħi 7 v . cot . cū . iiii . caʰr . Ibi æccɫa 7 ii . ſerui.

T . R . E . uaɫƀ . c . ſoɫ . Poſt ʰ l . ſoɫ . Modo ʰ iiii . liƀ.

In WOTTON Hundred

2 Ralph holds WESTCOTT himself. Abbot Alfsi*held it from King Edward.
Then it answered for 10 hides, now for 3 hides.
Land for 7 ploughs. In lordship 1 plough;
  14 villagers and 5 smallholders with 7 ploughs. 3 slaves.
  A mill at 30d; meadow, 2½ acres; woodland at 30 pigs.
Value before 1066 £9; later and now £8.

33 LAND OF ALFRED OF MARLBOROUGH* 36d

In WOKING Hundred

1 Alfred holds SEND from the King, and Reginald from him.
Karl held it before 1066. Then and now it answered for 20 hides.
Land for 10 ploughs. In lordship 2 ploughs, and 8 slaves;*
  14 villagers and 10 smallholders with 6 ploughs.
  A mill which pays 21s 6d. A church; 5 fisheries which pay 54d;
    meadow, 100 acres less 16; woodland at 160 pigs.
Of this land Walter holds 1½ hides, and Herbert 9, of
villagers' land. In lordship 2 ploughs, and 7 slaves;
  1 villager and 16 smallholders.
  A mill which pays 2s.
Total value before 1066 £20; now, the lordship £10, the rest 110s.

34 LAND OF ALBERT

In WALLINGTON Hundred

1 Albert the Clerk holds ADDINGTON from the King. Osward held it
from King Edward. Then it answered for 8 hides, now for 2.
Land for 4 ploughs. In lordship 2 ploughs;
  5 villagers and 4 cottagers with 1½ ploughs.
  Woodland, 20 pigs.
[Value] before 1066 and now 100s.

35 LAND OF ODARD

In ELMBRIDGE Hundred

1 Odard the Gunner* holds 4 hides from the King in ESHER. Tovi
held from King Edward. Now it answers for 1 hide.
  10 villagers with 2 ploughs.
  Meadow, 2 acres.
Value 40s.

2 Odard also holds (West) MOLESEY. Tovi held it from King Edward.
Then it answered for 6 hides and 1 virgate, now for 1 hide.
Land for 3 ploughs. In lordship 1;
  10 villagers and 5 cottagers with 4 ploughs. A church; 2 slaves.
Value before 1066, 100s; later 50s; now £4.

TERRÆ OSWOLDI 7 ALIOᵹ TAINOᵹ. IN FINGEHÁ HVND.

Oswold ten de rege PECHINGEORDE .Ipſe tenuit de rege.E.

Tc 7 m̃ ſe deſđ ꝓ una hida.Tra.ē.iii..caŕ.In dñio.ē una caŕ.7 iii.uiłłi
7 ii.borđ cũ.ii.caŕ.Ibi.ii.ſerui.   T.R.E.7 poſt.7 m̃.ual xl.ſoł.
Hõēs epi Baiocſis calũniant̃ ſuꝑ hanc tr̃a ad op̃ ꝛegis ꝑ ſingłos annos
ii.mark auri.uel.ii.accipitres.7 hoc ꝑ ccceſſionē abbis fr̃is Oſuuoldi.
Scilicet ꝓ bello qđ cont̃ Gaufriđ paruũ facere debuit.

In COPEDEDORNE HVNĐ ten Seman uña v̾ træ.qũa tenuit de rege.E.
Sed ex quo uen̾.W.rex in anglĩa.̾ ſeruiuit Oſuuoldo.redđ ei.xx.den̾.
Hic ſe potuit uertere quo uoluit T.R.E.

Ipſe Oſuuold ten FECEHÁ.Ipſe tenuit de rege.E.Tc ſe deſđ ꝓ xi.hiđ.
modo ꝓ iii.hiđ.Tra.ē   In dñio.ē una caŕ.7 xii.uiłłi 7 vi.borđ
cũ.v.caŕ.De molin̄ vi.ſoł 7 vi.den̾.Ibi.x.ãc p̃ti.Silua.de.iiii.porc̾.
T.R.E.ualb.iiii.lib.Modo.̾c.ſoliđ.   IN WODETON HĐ.

Ipſe Oſuuold ten ODETONE.Herald tenuit T.R.E.ſed dñt hõēs de
hunđ q̃a neſciunt quom̃ Herald habuit.Tc ſe deſđ ꝓ.vi.hiđ.Modo.̾
ꝓ.v.hiđ.Tra.ē   In dñio.ē una caŕ.7 xx.uiłłi 7 vii.borđ.cũ
viii.caŕ 7 dim̃.Ibi uñ molin̄ de.xx.denaŕ.7 iii.ãc p̃ti.Silua.de.l.porc̾.
De herbagio.xxiii.porc̾.T.R.E.7 poſt.ualuit.viii.lib.Modo.̾vii.lib
De his hiđ ten Ricarđ de Tonebrige.i.hid̃a.7 Corbelin de eo.
Tedric tenuit de Heraldo ꝓ uno m̃.Tc ſe deſđ ꝓ una hida.m̃ ꝓ dimiđ.
Ibi.ē dim̾caŕ.7 ii.uiłłi 7 uñ ſeruus.Valuit tc.xx.ſoł.Modo.̾x.ſoł.

Ipſe Oſuuold ten WISELEI.Ipſe tenuit de Heraldo IN WOCHINGES HĐ.
Tc ſe deſđ ꝓ.iii.hiđ 7 dim̃.Modo ꝓ una hida 7 dim̃.Tra.ē.ii.caŕ.

36   LAND OF OSWALD AND OTHER THANES

In EFFINGHAM Hundred

1 Oswald holds 'PITCHINGWORTH' from the King. He held it himself
from King Edward. Then and now it answers for 1 hide.
Land for 3 ploughs. In lordship 1 plough;
   3 villagers and 2 smallholders with 2 ploughs. 2 slaves.
Value before 1066, later and now 40s.
   The Bishop of Bayeux's men claim against this land 2 marks* of
gold or 2 hawks for the King's work each year: this by
consent of the Abbot, Oswald's brother,* namely for a combat*
which he ought to have fought against Geoffrey* the Little.

In COPTHORNE Hundred

2 Saeman holds 1 virgate of land which he held from King Edward.
But since King William came to England he has served Oswald
and paid him 20d. He could turn where he would before 1066.

3 Oswald holds FETCHAM himself. He held it himself from King Edward.
Then it answered for 11 hides, now for 3 hides. Land for ....
In lordship 1 plough;
   12 villagers and 6 smallholders with 5 ploughs.
   From a mill 6s 6d; meadow, 10 acres; woodland at 4 pigs.
Value before 1066 £4; now 100s.

In WOTTON Hundred

4 Oswald holds WOTTON himself. Harold held it before 1066, but
the men of the Hundred state that they do not know how Harold had it.
Then it answered for 6 hides, now for 5 hides. Land for ....
In lordship 1 plough;
   20 villagers and 7 smallholders with 8½ ploughs.
   A mill at 20d; meadow, 3 acres; woodland for 50 pigs;
     from grazing, 23 pigs.
Value before 1066 and later £8; now £7.
   Of these hides Richard of Tonbridge holds 1 hide, and Corbelin
from him. Theodoric held it from Harold as one manor.
Then it answered for 1 hide, now for ½. There is ½ plough there.
   2 villagers and 1 slave.
Value then 20s; now 10s.

In WOKING Hundred

5 Oswald holds WISLEY himself. He held it himself from Earl Harold.
Then it answered for 3½ hides, now for 1½ hides. Land for 2 ploughs.

In dñio.ē una.7 IIII.uilti 7 IIII.borđ cū.II.caŕ. Ibi æccła 7 II.ſerui.
7 uñ moliñ de.x.ſol.7 VI.ãc p̃ti.7 piſcaria de.v.denaŕ. Siluā.de.VI.
porc̃.   T.R.E.ualb̃ XL.ſol.Modo.́LX.ſol. *IN BRIXISTAN HĐ.*

Teodricvs aurifab̃ teñ de rege *Chenintvne*.Ipſe tenuit de rege.E.
Tc̃ ſe defđ ꝑ.v.hiđ.m̃ ꝑ una hida 7 III.uirḡ.Tra.ē.II.caŕ 7 dim̃.
In dñio.ē una caŕ.7 IIII.uilti 7 III.borđ cū.II.caŕ. Ibi uñ ſeruus.7 IIII.
ãc p̃ti. Valuit 7 ual.III.lib̃.   *IN W..LETON HVNĐ.*

Tezelin coquus teñ de rege *Edintone*.Godric tenuit de rege.E.Tc̃ ſe
defđ ꝑ.VIII.hiđ.m̃ ꝑ una hida.Tra.ē.IIII.caŕ. In dñio ſunt.II.caŕ.
7 VIII.uilti 7 IX.cot.cū.II.caŕ 7 dim̃.Silua.́de.xx.porc̃.Val 7 ualuit.c.ſol.
Ansgot ᶦⁿ ᵖʳᵉˢ teñ de rege *Cvbe*.Cola tenuit T.R.E. *IN CHINGESTVN HĐ.*
Tc̃ ſe defđ ꝑ.III.hiđ.m̃ ꝑ una hida 7 dim̃.Tra.ē.III.caŕ.In dñio.ē una.
7 VI.uilti 7 I.borđ cū.I.caŕ.7 IIII.ãc p̃ti.ꝑ herbagio.IIII.porc̃.Val.LX.ſol.
Chetel uenator teñ de rege *Lodesorde*.Pat ej *IN Wochinges HĐ.*
tenuit de rege.E.Tc̃ ſe defđ ꝑ una hida.m̃ ꝑ dimiđ.Tra.ē.II.caŕ.
In dñio.ē una. 7 II.uilti 7 v.borđ cū.I.caŕ.Moliñ de.II.ſol.7 IIII.ãc p̃ti.
Silua.́de.xx.porc̃. Val 7 ualuit.L.ſoliđ.

IN GODELAHNGE HVNĐ.

Wlwi uenator teñ de rege *Liteltone*.Ipſe tenuit de rege.E.Tc̃.II.hidæ
ſ; gſdū ñ deđ. Modo ꝑ una v̆.Tra.ē.I.caŕ. Ibi.ē in dñio.cū uno u l̃to
7 uno cot̃.cū una caŕ.Ibi.II.ãc p̃ti.Val 7 ualuit.xx.ſoliđ.

In lordship 1;
    4 villagers and 4 smallholders with 2 ploughs. A church; 2 slaves.
    A mill at 10s; meadow, 6 acres; a fishery at 5d; woodland at 6 pigs.
    Value before 1066, 40s; now 60s.

In BRIXTON Hundred
6 Theodoric the Goldsmith holds KENNINGTON from the King. He held
    it himself from King Edward. Then it answered for 5 hides, now
    for 1 hide and 3 virgates. Land for 2½ ploughs. In lordship 1 plough;
    4 villagers and 3 smallholders with 2 ploughs. 1 slave.
    Meadow, 4 acres.
    The value was and is £3.

In WALLINGTON Hundred
7 Tesselin Cook holds ADDINGTON from the King. Godric held it from
    King Edward. Then it answered for 8 hides, now for 1 hide.
    Land for 4 ploughs. In lordship 2 ploughs;
    8 villagers and 9 cottagers with 2½ ploughs.
    Woodland at 20 pigs.
    The value is and was 100s.

In KINGSTON Hundred
8 Ansgot the Interpreter holds COOMBE from the King. Cola held it
    before 1066. Then it answered for 3 hides, now for 1½ hides.
    Land for 3 ploughs. In lordship 1;
    6 villagers and 1 smallholder with 1 plough.
    Meadow, 4 acres; for grazing, 4 pigs.
    Value 60s.

In WOKING Hundred
9 Ketel Hunter holds LOLLESWORTH (?)* from the King. His father
    held it from King Edward. Then it answered for 1 hide, now for ½.
    Land for 2 ploughs. In lordship 1;
    2 villagers and 5 smallholders with 1 plough.
    A mill at 2s; meadow, 4 acres; woodland at 20 pigs.
    The value is and was 50s.

In GODALMING Hundred *
10 Wulfwy Hunter holds LITTLETON from the King. He held it himself
    from King Edward. Then 2 hides, but it did not pay tax; now for 1
    virgate. Land for 1 plough. It is there, in lordship, with
    1 villager and 1 cottager with 1 plough.
    Meadow, 2 acres.
    The value is and was 20s.

NOTES

ABBREVIATIONS used in the notes.

DB..Domesday Book. MS..Manuscript. EPNS..English Place Names Society.*
VCH .. Victoria County History.* PNDB .. O. von Feilitzen 'The Pre-Conquest Personal
Names of Domesday Book' Uppsala 1937.† OEB .. G. Tengvik 'Old English Bynames'
Uppsala 1938.†

* refers to the County volume, unless otherwise stated.   † 'Nomina Germanica,' volumes 3 and 4.

The manuscript is written on leaves, or folios, of parchment (sheep-skin), measuring about 15 inches
by 11 (38 by 28 cm), on both sides. On each side, or page, are two columns, making four to each
folio. The folios were numbered in the 17th century, and the four columns of each are here lettered
a,b,c,d. The manuscript emphasises words and usually distinguishes chapters and sections by the use
of red ink. Underlining indicates deletion.

L 6-11   ABBOT. Or 'Abbey'. In the text, chapter 12 has 'Abbey', for 'Abbess' in the List of
        Landholders; chapters 6-8 have 'Abbey', chapters 9-11 'Abbot'.

L 33   REGINALD... see 33,1 note.

1,1b   RANULF... probably Flambard.

1,1d,e   VILLAGE. Probably meaning Bramley.

1,2   IN LORDSHIP 1. Grammatically, persons as well as ploughs might be 'in lordship'.
        That is sometimes meant (see 33,1), but not normally. The punctuation draws attention
        to the ambiguity of the Latin.
        CHURCH. Churches, priests and slaves are sometimes grouped with people, sometimes
        with resources, sometimes elsewhere; a full stop here translates 'ibi'; a stop is also
        inserted between people and resources.

1,2   PIGS. In Surrey, the number paid for the right of pasturage. The payment was
        sometimes one pig in ten (1,6 and 19,11); sometimes, as in Sussex (e.g. 1,5,col.16c),
        one pig in seven (19,23 and 30,1). Here, the figure 133 suggests the Middlesex rate
        of one pig in three.

1,3   THE KING HOLDS. These words are repeated at the beginning of each of the
        sections 1,3 – 1,14.

1,3   40 PIGS; Farley prints '7' ('et', and). The MS sign is probably a badly formed
        ampersand (&), but might be intended for 'autem' or 'tamen' ('but').

1,4   ANSWERED. In Surrey, many hide assessments were reduced, often drastically.
        Some reductions may be due to damage done in the campaign of 1066; but the
        values are rarely reduced on a corresponding scale, and in some instances (e.g. 1,9) a
        different reason is explicitly stated. In some districts, the 1066 assessment seems over
        large, at 120 acres to the hide.
        NEW...CHURCH. Probably the Cluniac Church of St. Saviour's, founded by
        Alwin of London in 1082 (Bermondsey Chronicle).
        1 HIDE. See 17,2.

1,5   SULUNG. 'Solin', the Kentish equivalent of the 'hide'.

1,8   In-GOING. 'Releva' ('relief'), payment made to the King or Lord on a change of
        landholder, commonly by inheritance; in the 11th century sometimes reckoned as a
        quarter of the value.

1,9   2 HIDES AND 1 VIRGATE. The difference between the 1066 and 1086 assessments.

1,13   THREE MANORS. Four are listed (1,7; 1,10; 1,12-13); Reigate (1,7), held 'now for
        the King's work', was perhaps excluded.

2,3   8...HIDES. Presumably at Barnes, see 13,1.

3,1   1 HIDE. At Bentley (SU 78 44), four miles from Farnham, see Hampshire 2,25 (40 d).

4   BISHOP OSBERN. Of Exeter.

5,1a   100 PIGS. The figure might be read as ci (101), but probably intends c (100).
        £ 40. 'sol' (shillings) underlined for deletion, corrected to 'lib' (pounds).

5,1c   2...HIDES. Probably at Clandon, see 8,29.

5,3   IN WALES. In 1081.
        TO KENT. Probably in 1082.

5,7   WHITFORD. Evidently reached by Whitford Lane, Mitcham, EPNS 52; compare
        Whitford Gardens, London Road. The ford presumably crossed the Wandle.

5,9	CHALDON. EPNS 42. Farley 'Salvedone', MS 'Calvedone', the initial being a long 'S' imperfectly corrected to a 'C'.
5,13	HUNDRED. Within each chapter, DB normally lists the holdings in each Hundred in a single group. In Surrey, this arrangement is disturbed in chapters 5,6,8 and 19. BATTERSEA. See 6,1.
5,14	STREATHAM. See EPNS 33 and 8,15 below.
5,17	HALF MILLS. See 5,17 and 5,22.
5,19	THEM. 'Hoc', understanding 'manerium'; in English, referring to the hides. ILBERT. Probably Ilbert of Lacy, large holder in Yorkshire and elsewhere.
5,22	SIXTH. MS 'vi'; Farley, in error, 'v'.
5,24	FOUR MANORS. Presumably the lands of the 3 free men of Burgh (5,24) with the hide in Esher (5,25).
5,26	THEY. 'habuer(at)' (he had not had) is possible, but unusual and improbable; the normal expansion should be 'habuer(unt)', as in 'tenuer(unt)' etc.. above. The probable meaning is that the sisters could not prove lawful possession.
5,28	SHORE...WATERFRONT. 'Strande..Vicus Aquae'. The basic meaning of 'vicus' is a group of houses, small town or urban district; the mediterranean meaning of 'street' was rare in England before the 13th century.
5,30	OUTLIERS. MS 'b' added above the line, probably for 'berewica'.
6,1	2 HIDES...LATER. Evidently at Peckham, see 5,13.
6,4	SWEIN. Possibly Swein of Essex; 'kinsman of King Edward', Kemble 'Codex Diplomaticus' 846 = F.E. Harmer 'Anglo-Saxon Writs' 92, p.357, pp.311 ff.
7,1	21 VILLAGERS. 'Vill(anu)s' (singular) for 'vill(an)i' (plural). The grammatical eccentricity also occurs in 8,3 and 22,1, in each case after the figure 'xxi'.
8,3	21 VILLAGERS. See 7,1.
8,5	IN...ITSELF. This marginal insertion is placed between columns c and d of folio 32, leaving a clear space in the MS on the left, opposite 8,4, and intruding into the alignment of 8,16 (Esher, in Elmbridge Hundred), on the right. Farley's printed lay-out rightly connects with the left hand column, and the entry for Tandridge Hundred (8,4), where no place is named.
8,15	HAM. 'Estreham', the same spelling as for Streatham in Brixton Hundred (5,14). The only 'Ham' known in Kingston Hundred is Ham by Richmond; 'estre' may here mean 'eowestre' (sheep fold, or ewe fold), see EPNS 25 (Elements 1) pp. 155 and 160. A possible alternative is Ham, west of the mouth of the Wey, TQ 06 64(65), Chertsey land, but in Godley Hundred.
8,18	GODLEY HUNDRED. Here and in 8,19, written in the middle of the first line of the entry, not as a separate heading. The entries are placed between Effingham Hundred entries. Here, the omission of 8,20 was perhaps not observed until after the first words of 8,18 had been written; see 5,13. RECKLESS. '(E)Sturmid', probably from Old French 'etourdi' (heedless, reckless), OEB 345. Since the unusual name was also used by Radulfus (S)turmit (Norfolk 31,38, col. 252 b), possibly a relative, it had perhaps already become a family name.
8,19	GODLEY HUNDRED. See 8,18.
8,20	OSWALD. Perhaps the thane Oswald, brother of Abbot Wulfwold (ch. 36), who may also be the Oswald of 19,13 and 19,19. The entry may in part be duplicated in Oswald's Effingham holding in 19,44.
8,22	ODIN. So the MS. Farley, wrongly, 'Odm(us)'; see 19,2.
8,22	VALUE...60s. The entry is carried on from the end of col. 32 d to the beginning of 34 a, interrupted by the insertion of folio 33.
8,23-27	THESE ENTRIES were written across both columns of the first page of a folio, 33, inserted between 32 and 34. In this edition, each Latin line is set as two lines, an indentation marking the break thus introduced. In the MS, about half an inch was left between the first six lines (8,23-26) and the last two (8,27). Farley and the facsimile place these entries at the top of the page; the modern rebinding sets them about the middle of the page.
8,25	TOOTING. Perhaps Lower Tooting.
8,26	TOOTING. Perhaps Tooting Graveney.
8,29	CLANDON. Probably the hides of 5,1c.

11,1   BRANSHILL (?). Possibly a lost Surrey name. Either 'shelter (geselle) where broom grew', or, in Kentish dialect, 'Bramble Hill'. Branshill (Brembelshulle) (TQ 76 15, EPNS Sussex 496), now restricted to a farm name, is the English name for all or part of Battle Hill. Since one Surrey holding (18,1) was attached to a Sussex manor 25 or more miles distant before 1066, the site of Battle may have been attached to Limpsfield. If so, the grant of this single Surrey manor to the Abbey is readily explained.

13,1   MORTLAKE. See 2,3.
         10 VILLAGERS. Farley, 'ix vill(an)i'; MS 'x', with a long initial looped tail, probably intending '10', but possibly an imperfect correction of 'x' to 'ix'.

14,1   COUNTESS GODA. Died 1056; Countess of Boulogne.
         FIELD. 'Cultura'; see, e.g., Cheshire (South Lancashire) R 2,2 (col. 269 d) 'metebant in culturis regis' (they reaped in the King's fields).

15,2   WALKINGSTEAD. Corresponding to modern Godstone, EPNS 317,320.

16,1   COUNTESS OF BOULOGNE. Ida of Lorraine, second wife of Count Eustace.

17,1   LAMBETH. Probably Stockwell and South Lambeth; see the boundaries in Kemble 'Codex Diplomaticus' 813 (p. 158).

17,2   BERMONDSEY. See 1,4.

17,4   HAM. The only known Ham in Wallington Hundred is Ham in Croydon, EPNS 51.

18,1   SUSSEX. See Sussex 11,36 (col. 24 a).

19,2   ODIN. See 8,22. The MS might here be read as 'Odm(us)', but no such name is known.
         LEOFMER. MS 'Lemei', in error for 'Lemer'; 'Le(o)dmer' (21,2) is a possible alternative.

19,6   MANOR. Possibly Warlingham in Tandridge Hundred; see VCH 315.

19,10   BEC. Bec-Hellouin (Eure) 20 miles north-west of Evreux.
         1 HIDE. Inserted above the line as a correction, the long downward stroke intended as a deletion mark against 'similiter'.

19,11   1 HIDE AND 1 VIRGATE OF LAND. Correction and deletion, as in 19,10.

19,13   WORTH. Probably in Sussex, just across the modern county boundary; but possibly a lost Surrey 'Worth'.

19,20   HIDES. Followed by a gap, sufficient for the 1086 assessment; left blank because 19,21 gives a combined assessment for both places.
         ROD. Possibly 'v(irga)' rather than 'v(irgata)'.

19,22   LAND. 'Terram', not classified as a manor.
         'IMMERWORTH'. Ember (Court) in Thames Ditton, EPNS 91, on the borders of Kingston and Elmbridge Hundred, to which it later belonged.

19,25   TO RICHARD. Rather than 'against Richard', as VCH 317.

19,27   [PLOUGHS]. MS 'vi cot cum iiii cot', in error for 'vi cot cum iiii car'.
         6 PIGS. The 'v' of 'vi' is written over a previous figure, perhaps 'i'.

19,34-35 DIRTHAM. See EPNS 102.

19,35   CLAIMS. Farley 'calu(m)niatt', with an abbreviation sign over the first two letters 't'; so MS, but with overwriting, which extends into the space before the following word, and perhaps mistakenly alters 'calumniat' to 'calumniant'.
         2 HIDES. Those of 19,34 and 19,35.

19,37   ROBERT. Probably of Watteville.

19,39   2 HIDES. Those of Alric and Aelmer, and of Merwin; Merwin's holding is given first as 1 hide and 1 virgate, later as 1 hide.

19,40-43 FOUR ENTRIES added at the foot of the column, which were not Richard's lands.

19,41   MIDEHAM. Either a lost place, or a misreading of 'Micleham' (Mickleham) in the return copied.

19,43   2 HIDES. Probably at Milton, see 21,4.

19,46   WOTTON HUNDRED. The Hundred heading is misplaced, after instead of before Ockley. ½ HIDE. 'Hida' for 'hida(m)', the abbreviation sign omitted.

21,1   WHITFORD. See 5,7.

21,2   LEDMER. Or possibly Leofmer, see 19,2.

21,3   HELDRED. Perhaps for Aldred.

21,4   2 HIDES...THIS MANOR. Probably the hides of 19,43.

21,6-7   GUARD. 'Huscarle', King's Household Guard, not uncommon as a personal name.

22,1   21 VILLAGERS. 'xxi villan(u)s', see 7,1 and 8,3.

23; 24   THESE CHAPTERS, in small lettering, are squeezed into a space too small for them; see also chapter 26. The misplaced entry (22,5) is transcribed in normal lettering.

24,1   [GODALMING HUNDRED]. Farley's print gives the misleading impression that space
was left for the missing Hundred heading. In the MS, the chapter title is written in that
space, not above it.

25,1   DOES NOT BELONG. 'P(er)tinet', not 'pertinuit', meaning that it does not belong to
the land which was Asgar's. Two oblique strokes in the left margin of the MS, running
down from left ro right, may be intended to mark disputed tenure.
ASGAR. The Constable (Stalre), much of whose land was granted to Geoffrey.

25,2   27 HIDES. The figures detailed total 26 hides.

25,3   BROTHERS. Possibly Harold's brothers.

26   THIS CHAPTER is entered in small lettering, as chapters 23 and 24.

22,5   THIS MISPLACED ENTRY is assigned to its proper place by transposition marks, in
the right margin at its proper place, the left margin at its actual place. Farley's printed
rosettes represent a simple circle with a vertical line running through and below it in
the MS.

27,5   FOR 5 HIDES...5 PIGS. Written as one line across the bottom of the whole page at the
foot of col. 36 a and b; here reproduced as two lines, the second indented.
THE VALUE...60s. Written at the foot of col. 36 b, to the right of the column.

29,1   MANOR. Farley prints a blank space; in the MS, four or five letters are erased.

29,2   CHESSINGTON. Later in Copthorne Hundred.
WIGOT. Of Wallington, father-in-law of Miles Crispin.

30,1   GODTOVI. MS 'Goltovi', for 'Godtovi', see 20, 1-2.
SEVENTH PIG. See 1,2.

31,1   [EDWARD]. Read 'de rege [E]'.

32,1   ABBOT ALFSI. Of Ramsey, perhaps also of St. Augustine's, Canterbury; 'Aethelsige'
in older spelling.

33   ALFRED OF MARLBOROUGH. In the List of Landholders Reginald's name is entered.

33,1   SLAVES. Here, and in the land held from Alfred, slaves are entered between lordship
ploughs and villagers, instead of in the position normal in Surrey, with the church,
before the mills and meadows. As normally, the Latin does not distinguish between
what is and is not in lordship; the word order suggests that in this entry the slaves were
regarded as in lordship, with the ploughs, in contrast with the villagers.

35,1   GUNNER. 'Balistarius'. The term 'ballista' comprehended all kinds of missile-throwing
weapons, from the crossbow to the large artillery piece. The English word 'gun' was
used of such weapons before the introduction of 'gun-powder'.

36,1   MARKS. Of gold, normally valued at £6; of silver, normally at 13s 4d.
ABBOT, OSWALD'S BROTHER. Abbot Wulfwold of Chertsey, died 1084; see 8,20.
COMBAT. 'Bellum', meaning judicial combat.
GEOFFREY. 'Gaufridus', an occasional variant of the more usual 'Goisfridus';
Geoffrey is not otherwise known.

36,9   LOLLESWORTH (?). 'Lodesorde'. Possibly Lodsworth near Midhurst (EPNS Sussex 26);
but perhaps a misspelling of Lollesworth in West Horsley in Woking Hundred (EPNS Surrey
141); compare Lowleth (Lolleworth) in Chertsey, in Godley Hundred (EPNS 381). For
confusion between 'Lod-' and 'Lol-' see, e.g., Hunts. 19,19.

36,10   IN GODALMING HUNDRED is entered in col. 36 c, opposite the last line of 36,9. The
first line of the entry, here shown as two lines with an indent, is written across both
columns in a single line at the foot of the page; the second line is at the foot of col. 36 c.

In the MS and in Farley, all chapter numbers are written to the left of the
column. In this edition, a few of the later and longer chapter numbers have
had to be placed above the chapters for reasons of space.

INDEX OF PERSONS

Familiar modern spellings are given when they exist. Unfamiliar names are usually given in an approximate late 11th century form, avoiding variants that were already obsolescent or pedantic. Spellings that mislead the modern eye are avoided where possible. Two, however, cannot be avoided; they are combined in the name 'Leofgeat', pronounced 'Leffyet,' or 'Levyet.' The definite article is omitted before bynames, except where there is reason to suppose that they described the individual. The chapter numbers of listed landholders are printed in italics.

Churches and Clergy

Archbishop of Canterbury   2
   see Lanfranc, Stigand
Bishop of Bayeux   *5.* 1,1c-d; 5; 11;
     13. 6,1. 8,29.
     14,1. 36,1
   of Exeter, see Osbern
of   of Lisieux   1,5. 5,10; 13. 6,1
   of Winchester   3
     see Walkelin
   Osbern   4
Abbess of Barking   12
Abbot of Battle   11
   of Chertsey   *8.* 6,1. (36,1)
     see Wulfwold
   of St. Leufroy   10
   of Ramsey, see Alfsi

   of St. Wandrille   9
   of Westminster   *6.* 19,40
   of Winchester   7
Canons of Bayeux   5, 6-7
   of St. Paul's   *13.* 2,3
   of Waltham   17,1; 4
Church of Lambeth   14
Saint Augustine's (Canterbury) see Alfsi
   Mary's of Bec   19,10
     see Lambeth
   Paul's (London) see Canons
   Peter's of Chertsey, see Abbot
   Peter's of Winchester, see Bishop
Clerks..Albert, Ranulf
Monk...Ingulf
Priest...Gilbert

Secular Titles and Occupational Names

Boy *(boi)*...Alwin. Chamberlain *(camerarius)*...Humphrey, William. Cook *(cocus)*...Tesselin. Count *(comes)*...Eustace (of Boulogne); Gilbert; of Mortain. Countess *(comitissa)*...Goda; (Ida) of Boulogne. Earl *(comes)*...Godwin, Harold, Roger, Leofwin, Waltheof. Goldsmith *(aurifaber)*...Theodoric. Gunner *(balistarius)*...Odard. Hunter *(venator)*...Aelmer, Colman, Ketel, Wulfwy. Interpreter *(interpres)*...Ansgot. Queen *(regina)*...Edith, (Matilda). Reeve *(prepositus; prefectus)* 1,1d-e;5;9. 6,1...Lufa, Tovi. Sheriff *(vicecomes)* 1,2-4; 6; 11; 13. 4,2. 21,3... Ansculf, Hamo, Ranulf. Vinedresser *(vinitor)*...Walter. Young *(cild)*...Alnoth, Brictsi.

INDEX OF PLACES

The name of each place is followed by (i) the initial of its Hundred and its location on the Map in this volume; (ii) its National Grid reference; (iii) chapter and section references in DB. Bracketed figures denote mention in sections dealing with a different place. Unless otherwise stated, the identifications of the English Place Names Society and the spellings of the Ordnance Survey are followed for places in England; of OEB for places abroad. A star (*) marks places outside Surrey. The National Grid reference system is explained on all Ordnance Survey maps, and in the Automobile Association Handbooks; the figures reading from left to right are given before those reading from bottom to top of the map. Starred grid references are in the 100 kilometer square lettered SU; others are in square TQ. The Surrey Hundreds are Brixton (B); Blackheath (Bh); Copthorne (C); Effingham (e); Elmbridge (E); Farnham (F); Godalming (G); Godley (Gy); Kingston (K); Reigate (R); Tandridge (T); Wallington (W); Woking (Wk); Wotton (Wt).

Places not named

In BLACKHEATH Hundred 5,1f. In COPTHORNE 5, 16-17; 19,40; 19,43; 21,4; 36,2.
In ELMBRIDGE 1,16; 8,7; 19,18; 19,33. In GODALMING 1,14. In KINGSTON 8,12.
In TANDRIDGE 8,4-5; 19 6. In WALLINGTON 5,12; 5,18; 8,23-24; 12,2; 14,1; 17,3; 23,1.
In WOTTON 1,11-12; 5,1d-e; 18,1. HUNDRED not stated 1,5.

Places not in Surrey
Places indexed above are starred; for others see Index of Persons.

Elsewhere in Britain.
BERKSHIRE Windsor*. DEVON Exeter, see Bishop Osbern. ESSEX Barking, see Abbess;
Waltham, see Canons. HAMPSHIRE 3,1; Winchester, see Abbot, Bishop. KENT 1,5-6,
see Hamo. Canterbury, see Archbishop, Abbot; Tonbridge, see Richard. MIDDLESEX
London* (see also Alnoth, St. Paul's); Westminster, see Abbot. SUSSEX 18,1; Battle, see
Abbot; Branshill;* Compton*; Worth*. WILTSHIRE Marlborough, see Alfred; Salisbury,
see Edward.

Places outside Britain
Abe(r)non, see Roger. L'Aigle, see Gilbert. Bayeux, see Bishop, Canons. Bec, see St. Mary's.
Boulogne, see Eustace, Goda. Braose (Briouze), see William. Douai, see Walter. Eu, see
Osbern. Mandeville, see Geoffrey. Oilly, see Robert. Port (-en Bessin), see Hugh. Rots, see
Ansketel. St. Leufroy, see Abbot. St. Wandrille, see Abbot. Watteville (Vatteville), see
Robert, William.

SYSTEMS OF REFERENCE TO DOMESDAY BOOK

The manuscript is divided into numbered chapters, and the chapters into sections, usually
marked by large initials and red ink. Farley however did not number the sections. References
have therefore been inexact, by folio numbers, which cannot be closer than an entire page or
column. Moreover, half a dozen different ways of referring to the same column have been
devised. In 1816 Ellis used three separate systems in his indices; (i) on pages i-cvii; 435-518;
537-570; (ii) on pages 1-144; (iii) on pages 145-433 and 519-535. Other systems have since
come into use, notably that used by Vinogradoff, here followed. This edition numbers the
sections, the normal practicable form of close reference; but since all discussion of Domesday
for three hundred years has been obliged to refer to page or column, a comparative table will
help to locate references given. The five columns below give Vinogradoff's notation, Ellis'
three systems, and that employed by Welldon Finn and others. Maitland, Stenton, Darby and
others have usually followed Ellis (i).

Vinogradoff	Ellis (i)	Ellis (ii)	Ellis (iii)	Finn
152a	152	152a	152	152 ai
152b	152	152a	152.2	152 a2
152c	152b	152b	152b	152 bi
152d	152b	152b	152b.2	152 b2

In Surrey, the relation between the Vinogradoff column notation, here followed, and the
chapters and sections is

30 a	1,1-1,2	32 a	5,22 - 5,29	35 a	19,15 - 19,24
b	1,2 - 1,7	b	6,1 - 7,1	b	19,24 - 19, 34
c	1,8 - 1,13	c	7,1 - 8,10	c	19,35 - 19,42
d	1,13 - 2,3	d	8,12 - 8,22	d	19,43 - 21,3
31 a	2,3 - 4,1	33 a,b	8,23 - 8,27	36 a	21,3 - 22,4; 23,1
b	4,1 - 5,3	c,d	blank page	b	22,5; 24,1 - 27,3
c	5,3 - 5,11	34 a	8,21 - 14,1	c	28,1 - 32,2
d	5,11 - 5,22	b	14,1 - 18,1	d	33,1 - 36,10
		c	18,2 - 19,4		
		d	19,4 - 19,15		

TECHNICAL TERMS

Many words meaning measurements have to be transliterated. But translation may not dodge other problems by the use of obsolete or made-up words which do not exist in modern English. The translations here used are given in italics. They cannot be exact; they aim at the nearest modern equivalent. Words of uncertain or arguable meaning are marked with a star (*).

BORDARIUS. Cultivator of inferior status, usually with a little land. *smallholder*

CARUCA. A plough, with the oxen who pulled it, usually reckoned as 8. *plough*

CILT.* *Childe*, an honourable appellation. *Young*

COTARIUS. Inhabitant of a *cote*, cottage, often without land. *cottager*

DOMINICUS.* Belonging to a lord or lordship. *the lord's* or *household*

DOMINIUM.* The mastery or dominion of a lord *(dominus)*; including ploughs, land, men, villages, etc., reserved for the lord's use; often concentrated in a *home farm* or *demesne*, a 'Manor Farm' or 'Lordship Farm'. *lordship*

FEUDUM.* Continental variant of *feuum*, not used in England before 1066; either a landholder's total holding, or land held by special grant. *Holding*

FEUUM. Old English *feoh*, cattle, money, possessions in general, compare Latin *pecunia* and German *Vieh*; in later centuries, *feoff*, 'fief' or 'fee'. *holding*

FIRMA. Old English *feorm*, provisions due to the King; a fixed sum paid in place of these and of other miscellaneous dues. *revenue*

GELDUM. The principal royal tax, originally levied during the Danish wars, normally at an equal number of pence on each *hide* of land. *tax*

HIDE.* A unit of land measurement, reckoned at 120 acres, but often different in practice; a unit of tax assessment, often differing from the cultivated hides. *hide*

HUNDRED. A district within a shire, who assembly of notables and village representatives usually met about once a month. *Hundred*

PRAEPOSITUS, PRAEFECTUS. Old English *gerefa*, a royal officer. *reeve*

SACA.* German *Sache*, English *sake*, Latin *causa*, affair, lawsuit; the fullest authority normally exercised by a lord. *full jurisdiction*

SOCA.* 'Soke', from *socn*, to seek, comparable with Latin *quaestio*. Jurisdiction, with the right to receive fines and a multiplicity of other dues. District in which such *soca* is exercised; a place in a *soca*. *jurisdiction*

SOCMANNUS.* 'Soke man', liable to attend the court of a *soca* and serve its lord; free from many villagers' burdens; before 1066 often with more land and higher status than villagers (see, e.g., Middlesex, Appendix); bracketed in the Commissioners' brief with the *liber homo* (free man). *Freeman*

TAINUS, TEGNUS. Person holding land from the King by special grant; in former times used of the King's chief ministers and companions. *thane*

T.R.E. *tempore regis Edwardi*, in King Edward's time. *before 1066*

VILLA. Translating Old English *tun*, town. The later distinction between a small *village* and a large *town* was not yet in use in 1066. *village*

VILLANUS. Member of a *villa*. *villager*

VIRGATA. A fraction of a *hide*, usually a quarter, notionally 30 acres. *virgate*

BRIXTON Hundred
1 Southwark
2 Lambeth
3 Bermondsey
4 Walworth
5 Kennington
6 Barnes
7 Battersea
8 Camberwell
9 Peckham
10 Hatcham
11 Mortlake
12 Putney
13 Wandsworth
14 Clapham
15 Balham
16 Tooting
17 Tooting Bec
18 Streatham
19 Merton

BLACKHEATH Hundred
1 Shalford
2 Chilworth
3 Albury
4 Shere
5 Gomshall
6 Bramley

COPTHORNE Hundred
1 Cuddington
2 Ewell
3 Epsom
4 Pachevesham
5 Ashtead
6 Burgh
7 Leatherhead
8 Tadworth
9 Fetcham
10 Thorncroft
11 Walton-on-the-Hill
12 Headley
13 Mickleham

EFFINGHAM Hundred
1 Little Bookham
2 Great Bookham
3 Effingham
4 Dirtham
5 'Pitchingworth'

ELMBRIDGE Hundred
1 West Molesey
2 Apps
3 East Molesey
4 Walton-on-Thames
5 Weston
6 Weybridge
7 Esher
8 Cobham
9 Stoke d'Abernon

FARNHAM Hundred
1 Farnham

GODALMING Hundred
1 Compton
2 Loseley
3 Littleton
4 Rodsall
5 Hurtmore
6 Farncombe
7 Peper Harow
8 Godalming
9 Tuesley
10 Witley
11 Hambledon

GODLEY Hundred
1 Egham
2 Thorpe
3 Chertsey
4 Chobham
5 Byfleet
6 Pyrford

KINGSTON Hundred
1 Petersham
2 Ham
3 Coombe
4 Kingston
5 'Immerworth'
6 Thames Ditton
7 Long Ditton
8 Tolworth
9 Malden
10 Chessington
11 Claygate

REIGATE Hundred
1 Chipstead
2 Merstham
3 Gatton
4 Buckland
5 Reigate
6 Nutfield
7 Worth

TANDRIDGE Hundred
1 Farleigh
2 Chelsham
3 Warlingham
4 Tatsfield
5 Tillingdown
6 Woldingham
7 Titsey
8 Oxted
9 Limpsfield
10 Walkingstead
11 Chivington
12 Blechingley
13 Tandridge

WALLINGTON Hundred
1 Mitcham
2 Morden
3 Whitford
4 Ham
5 Cheam
6 Carshalton
7 Wallington
8 Beddington
9 Croydon
10 Sutton
11 Addington
12 Sanderstead
13 Banstead
14 Woodmansterne
15 Coulsdon
16 Waddington
17 Chaldon

WOKING Hundred
1 Wisley
2 Woking
3 Ockham
4 Send
5 Henley
6 Worplesdon
7 Sutton
8 Lollesworth
9 Burpham
10 West Clandon
11 East Clandon
12 West Horsley
13 East Horsley
14 Wyke
15 Stoke
16 Wanborough
17 Guildford
18 Tyting

WOTTON Hundred
1 Dorking
2 Betchworth
3 Paddington
4 Wotton
5 Westcott
6 Milton
7 Sutton
8 Abinger
9 Anstie
10 Hartshurst
11 Ockley

Not mapped
Copthorne Hundred, *Mideham* (see Mickleham)
Wotton Hundred, 'Littlefield'.

National Grid figures are shown on the map border

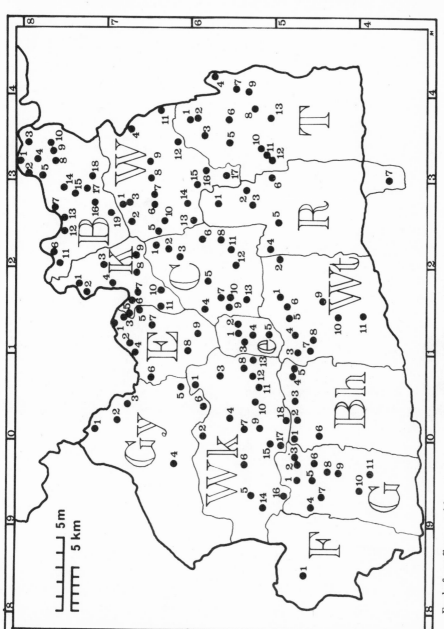

Each four-figure grid square represents one square kilometer, or 247 acres, approximately 2 hides, at 120 acres to the hide.

On the scale of this map, each dot is equivalent to about 100 acres.